C000214440

THE BRESSINGHAM STEAM SAGA

By the same author

Hardy Perennials & Alpines
Perennials for Trouble-free Gardening
Alpines for Trouble-free Gardening
The Farm in the Fen
The Fens
Skaters of the Fens
The Bressingham Story
A Plantsmans Perspective
Reeds in the Wind – *a Novel*
250 Years of Steam
Perennials for Your Garden

THE BRESSINGHAM STEAM SAGA

Alan Bloom

To Lou,
with good wishes from
Alan

Picton Publishing (Chippenham) Limited
CHIPPENHAM

First published in 1992
by Picton Publishing (Chippenham) Limited
ISBN 0 948251 56 5

Cover Design by
Jane Brett of MIJA Design
Set in Linotype Imprint by
Mike Kelly Phototypesetting,
Biddestone, Chippenham, Wiltshire SN14 7EA
Printed and Bound in the United Kingdom by
Picton Publishing (Chippenham) Limited
Queensbridge Cottages,
Patterdown,
Chippenham,
Wiltshire SN15 2NS
Telephone: (0249) 443430

Contents

Dedication

To all those without whose help
and encouragement, especially in the early days,
the Museum could not have developed.

List of Illustrations

Rain or Shine – The Spirit of Bressingham.

CHAPTER ONE

THE LONG TWO MILE JOURNEY

Bronllwyd, for all her being sixty years old is photogenic. Two men and one woman stood a few yards away with cameras poised, but one after the other shuffled a little to obtain a clearer view. It was obvious to me that what hindered them were those people who stood or passed by between them and *Bronllwyd*. Then after a minute or two the space was clear and I smiled as three forefingers pressed the cameras' buttons all at once. One man smiled back at me and stuck his thumb upwards as a sign of achievement. Forty yards away there stood *Oliver Cromwell*, much younger than *Bronllwyd* and twenty times her size and weight, but equally photogenic. And over there half hidden from my view was Bertha gently operating a threshing machine, just to let the visitors see the kind of work she was built to do. *Bronllwyd* was native to Leeds; *Oliver* to Crewe; but Bertha came from nearby Thetford.

With an eye now and then on either the vital gauges for water level and steam pressure, I once again had the strange feeling of unreality. It would have been totally beyond my imagining to have foreseen what was just a farmyard thirty years ago, to be thronged with people – half of them with cameras. Steam engines had fascinated me as a small boy – but there was nothing unusual in that, and I used to stand for hours watching farm engines at work before combine harvesters came. Even owning an engine and having it thresh out grain in this very yard from my own stacks was beyond imagination. But it had come to pass.

On *Bronwllwyd*'s left was a patch of sward. It had been a small orchard netted in for poultry when I came to Bressingham in 1946. Within a few years it was converted, half for propagating frames and half for nursery buildings. But now the packing shed I'd built in 1948 had gone and the offices were converted to tearooms. And in the centre of the grassy patch stood a set of steam driven Galloping Horses, all gaily painted and with an organ playing a Sousa march as the wooden horses and cockerells pranced up and down. To one side and further back was a large building where a spinney had once been. It now housed several large locomotives, the *Royal Scot* amongst them, and a display of stationary industrial engines. And a story lay behind both the building and the relics it preserved, which needs to be brought up to date.

But any wonderment in my mind as to how and why all this display and activity came about vanished as from behind came a shrill platform whistle. Glancing back I saw that my little train was thereabouts full – five open trucks in which sat a hundred or more people. Eyes forward and with a shrill whistle from *Bronwllwyd* I gently opened the regulator. The curve ahead skirted a row of railway seats facing the Roundabouts. The 2-foot track was not fenced, and with a down gradient a cautious walking pace was imperative. In over twenty years no one had ever been hurt or much less run over, but safety first was paramount. The train behind began to push *Bronwllwyd* and the steam brake was pulled on to take the strain as it passed the corner of the locomotive museum and workshop.

On the other side was a ramshackle wooden shed which old Jack Clements and I built when narrow gauge first came in 1965. Now it housed spares and supplies. Because of the gradient of 1 in 50, and because of people wandering towards or from the 15 inch Waveney Valley Railway, I had to be tensely alert with only a swift glance across the 2 acre lake I made in the 1950's. The excuse for making it was to serve as an irrigation reservoir; the real reason was a fondness for water as a scenic and recreational amenity.

Once safely over the points and where the two gauges crossed I could relax. As hoped and planned, one train was in the Lakeside Station on the left whilst the other glided in to the arrival platform on the right. It had completed the 2½ mile circuit and I was all set to drive *Bronwllwyd* at a leisurely 8 m.p.h. over a similar distance but a very different route. Rounding the first curve into an eastward straight in the shade of a leafy alder and willow grove, it was time to shovel coal on to the fire. Winds seldom came from the east to blow smoke over the passengers, and firing here would ensure there was little left on arrival back at the station. Not that passengers were annoyed by smoke. Some even said they liked to sniff it, remarking on how much more acceptable it was than diesel fumes.

It was along this stretch that I really got the hang of track-laying. This valley bottom was sandy here and peaty there and the two mixed to pack firmly. Levelling it off, and with heaps of railway sleepers sawn in half at intervals, I could leave them firmly bedded ready for my helpers to lay the second-hand rails. Friendly competition arose as they tried as hard as they could to catch up with me, whilst I tried to keep well ahead of them. That was in 1967 when the first extension from half a mile to a mile and a half was made. Two years later we laid a new line of similar length down to the woods and over the little Waveney river, but by 1972 the Woodland Railway had to be merged with the new venture into 15 inch after rushing over to Cologne to buy the two Krupps locomotives and eighteen coaches.

Now, more relaxed, memories emerged from the sight of ditches which had to be dug to fight the menace of floods – a fight I'd not always won, of poplar trees I'd planted on land too wet for other crops, proven by trial and loss. Past a thicket where alder trees had grown from seeds lying dormant in soil spread from a new ditch. And skirting a 20 acre pasture which turf digging had left derelict for me to reclaim, I blew *Bronwllwyd*'s whistle again. Ahead was a crossing, shaped like half open scissors and I had right of way as the Waveney Line driver well knew. But as he slowed down, the custom was well established for the Nursery Line train to cross first and then itself slow down so that passengers on each could see the passing of the other. Some waved, some clicked cameras and some, I'd reckoned artfully, would be encouraged to ride on both routes. Such timing was fortuitous and it worked whether one or two trains were running on each line. The scissor crossing was in a little grove of oaks and birches. They were the only trees worth leaving on a 12 acre rabbit infested waste of brambles and gorse when a neighbour and I decided that, since no owner existed, we would claim and clear it. After twelve years, according to law, it would be ours by right, 6 acres each. Now, Freezen Hills – or Free Sand Hills – was part of the nursery with buildings and frames for the herbaceous Perennials section and the sandy hummocks levelled off on which specimen conifers were now growing.

Beyond, the open fields to the east sloped up to Roydon, topped by the round tower of St Eligius' Church beside a big Lebanon cedar. When easterly winds blew, they came cold off the North Sea forty miles away – or from the Arctic, for there were no hills high enough in Norfolk to hinder their power or take off their chill. As the track made a full bend northwards the wind would be checked by a row of trees planted in 1969 when the fourth extension to the route was made beside a large new ditch. Here the sandy soil had changed to the most obdurate clayey stuff I'd ever encountered and track laying in a wet spell had been very hard work. But if these trees were a windbreak, they overhung the track so that in rainy weather their leaves shed heavy drops on to *Bronwllwyd* and me from her chimney exhaust, bringing them down.

Nonetheless, I prefer driving a cabless engine in order to see around and even chat occasionally to passengers in the front seat behind me. Near a big willow *Bronwllwyd* lurches where a tree root persists in heaving up the track. But then she lurches at the least provocation over much of the route, for though she has three sets of wheels they are close together and the weight fore and aft accentuates any unevenness. More conifers, more nursery beds and frames on either side as we head west. On the right a low building houses a pump, but passengers cannot guess that it draws water from a borehole 150 feet deep. Sand and clay were penetrated and chalk reached at 70 feet. From well into the chalk, streams of water under pressure force it up to the surface and after pumping all day it wells up to the top again unfailingly. But for the assurance of a good water supply I would never have bought Bressingham Hall Farm. As it was, there were so many hindrances to sinking the first artesian borehole following the terrible winter of 1946–7 in which the nursery had to be moved from Oakington, near Cambridge that this became one of several reasons why my children and I took off to Canada in 1948. My father thought this a very foolhardy venture, and returning home nearly broke in 1950 proved his opinion well founded. It was the biggest blunder I ever made, but at least it taught me a lesson. Hard times followed, for everything left behind had been neglected by those I'd trusted. What angered me most was the loss of *Bella* – the first traction engine I had ever owned, worked with and loved for all her waywardness.

Taking a short up gradient of 1 in 36 with only an extra loud bark from her chimney, *Bronwllwyd* rounded another curve so that passengers could see rows of 'poly tunnels' full of young plants and beyond a set of buildings including one big shed covering nearly half an acre. That's the potting shed, I sometimes told them, whilst my mind flashed back to the early days when a hen hut had to do for potting. Slowing down a little, passengers could see acres of beds in which potted plants are grown – by the million – for under my two sons' control the nursery has become the largest of its type in Britain employing over 200 people. Behind a dense hedge is the latest development of a retail sales centre covering 5 acres on which a wide selection of the 2,500 kinds of plants we produce are offered. It had to come, but wholesaling had always been my personal preference. Ahead, in front of a chestnut tree under which the track disappeared was a large notice to whistle. It had to be more than just a pip because it warned those in charge of the departure platform that we were coming in, and it was time for the second train already there to leave as I'd done twelve minutes before. Gliding in to the arrival platform to a stop on my left is the largest of the museum buildings and the last to be built. Apart from an array of static engines, a Royal Coach and a gallery for Railwayana, there is a spaceous souvenir shop area and toilets of which we are justly proud. Such a building was badly needed and we'd muddled along for several years before I asked the Bank for a hefty loan with which to build it. But now the loan has been paid back, and if resources are still slender we are at least free and independent.

The other train having gone to leave the departure platform free, I had to wait for a passage with other people crossing the line just in front of *Bronwllwyd*. It was another time for alertness, and for a warning pip on the whistle. It was also a time when often a few of my disembarked passengers would come along to see the engine which had taken them. A couple with two young children came close. "Go on you two", said the man, "say thank you for a nice ride to the driver, because it's Mr Bloom himself who owns all this. I know it's him because of the photo of him in this engine in the guide book".

Somewhat overawed and sheepish the children did as they were bid. Liking the look of them, they were invited to stand beside me on the footplate whilst their father clicked his camera.

I couldn't tell them how it was that I was not the owner. For that was quite a long story and I had to move on to the next platform where fresh groups of passengers were waiting.

The author in contemplative mood.

CHAPTER TWO

A VILLAGE BOY'S WONDER

Old time threshing with a 'Portable' engine.

One of the peculiar attributes of steam is that when used as a source of power, it can fascinate so many who pause to watch it at work. Such people may not be in the least inquisitive, wishing to know how it works, how such an ordinary thing as boiling water can produce such power, much less on the intracacies of moving parts, – pistons, valves, cranks and what not, and those who find within themselves a response to the evocative magic of steam at an early age, it is almost certain to remain with them for life. So, with steam being phased out in favour of oil and electricity it takes on another quality or attribute – the power to generate nostalgia along with a renewal perhaps of childhood awe. Steam engines were commonplace when I was young, but in the Fenland village where I lived, they were not to be seen every day. Sometimes they could be heard a long way off – iron wheels on hard roads, and when taken for walks by a nursemaid she often pushed my younger brother and me into a muddy farm yard where an engine was at work. More often she would take us to Swavesey station on the Cambridge–St, Ives line in hopes of us seeing a train. There, looking east, it was dead straight to Longstanton and engine smoke could be spotted at least two miles away. To the west there was a curve and one of the most wonderful sights was that of a quite small 2–4–0 Midland twin-engine – an express because after St. Ives it was not allowed to pick up passengers on this Great Eastern line. The thrill was brief as the smart red engine flashed by non-stop to Cambridge. Later I saw one one held up and noted that it was built at Derby in 1879.

Road using engines were very different, and unlike the railway locomotives which on this line all had inside cylinders with moving rods and cranks unseen under the boiler barrel, all the moving parts of traction engines could be seen. And fascinating it was to watch these for hours as I became older and more free to wander as the fancy took me. These engines did not puff loudly like railway locomotives, and when threshing more noise was made by the drum into which sheaves of corn were thrown. Its sound was rather like a moan, rising and falling according to how the sheaves were spread as the feeder on top cut the strings. Then there was the slapping sound of the belts, a big one from the engine flywheel to a small one on the drum which in turn carried other smaller belts on the threshing drum itself. Behind it the elevator or straw jack made a regular click-clack noise as the straw spewed out from the drum to be carried in a trough up to the stack.

The engine rocked gently against the scotches under the big iron wheels. The rocking was as regular as the motion of the piston rod as it went in and out of the cylinder to drive the red painted crankshaft, to which the flywheel was fixed. These working parts made no sound, but often a musical clink came from

The steering gear of a Burrell Self Propelled Traction Engine.

the row of wheel spuds or cleats dangling from behind the coal bunker. And on this bunker, with the engine in charge of a friendly driver, I was sometimes allowed to sit to look down instead of up on to the moving parts. Coal dust was fairly easy to brush off my backside with a tuft of straw. I could also see, often in a haze of dust, the lad who had to stand in the narrow space between stack and drum hooking up empty chaff sacks and taking them away when full, feeling sorry for him as it was a filthy task regarded almost as a penance. The man at the grain end of the drum, filling corn sacks from little slotted openings had to be strong. Wheat at 18 stones barley at 16 and oats at 12 stone all went into a standard size sack. But they had to be placed on a weighing machine and then lifted on to a cart to be taken away. When no ratcheted sack-lifter was to hand, two men were needed to lift full sacks from ground level to the cart.

A threshing gang – up to ten men – had to work in with the machines. There was no place for slackers. Mostly they worked in silence, with an occasional shout when a rat tried to escape as the corn stack diminished. Boys such as I were encouraged to kill mice or rats with thatching spars but it was not unknown for a rat to make for a man's trouser leg. It made sense, the engine driver said, for those on the corn stack to tie their trouser bottoms tightly with binder string. The driver was usually the boss of the gang, responsible for efficient running. The owner of the set was a contractor and the farmer paid him either as piece work based on the yield or by the day and hour, and it was the farmer who had to provide coal and water for the engine as well as helpers other than the drum feeder.

Coal and water were the only two ingredients for all the power of steam engines. Fire made water boil to give off steam and to me it was a marvellous invention. Maybe it was because you could see the result – the magical process, whereas with a motor car there was nothing to see under the bonnet except a block with next to no moving parts. A steam engine stirred something deep inside one, held one's attention, evoked one's awe and wonder. It was not until years later that I reasoned out why this was so and why it affected so many people in the same way, and why boys such as I wanted to become engine drivers when they grew up. Not that I fancied driving a traction engine as a career, for they were so slow moving and never went more than a very few miles from their home base.

The two threshing sets that served the village were in competition. Some preferred Seamark's Fowell because it was newer and cleaner than Mustills's Marshall. It was Frank Parrish who drove the latter and allowed me to sit on the coal in the bunker and that was enough. Differences in make meant little and both had the same kind of moving parts as they worked. Frank showed me how he took it out of gear, which enabled the engine to work a threshing set by disengaging the cogs which drove the road wheels. Sometimes I could witness the procedure for using the winch holding a wire rope. It was housed behind one of the big driving wheels and when a heavy crosspin was withdrawn from the massive wheel hubs the winch could operate freely. It was often used when not even cleated wheel rims would grip in mud or on a slope, but the wire rope, steam power would pull the heavy threshing drum with very little effort over the most difficult conditions.

"It would pull a house down", Frank told me proudly and once I witnessed the next best thing, apart from seeing a sizeable tree pulled out with its roots. It was a large thatched barn not far from home. The owner needed the space it was said, and decided to use Frank's engine rather than dismantle it bit by bit. The wire rope was paid out with the engine back wheels firmly scotched till it encircled the barn with the hooked end coming back to be fixed on the engine. Boys were ordered to stand back and older onlookers saw to it that we did so as Frank gently opened the throttle. The slack on the rope slithered like a snake until it became taut and with the flywheel turning quite slowly still, cracking noises came from the big old timbered barn. The roof began to shudder as Frank pressed his lever a little more and the rope, two feet or so above ground twanged under the strain. And then, with almost a bark from the engine chimney, the barn collapsed in a cloud of dust and in less than a minute the roof and all the ancient timbers were in a jumbled heap on the ground.

"Steam's hully marvellous – nothing to beat it for power", a man remarked as Frank grinned and waved down from his engine to the little crowd, whilst lighting his pipe.

There was one other steam engine in Over which did not do contract work, nor could it move by itself. It belonged to Fred

Kirby, and horses were required to move it from one or the other of his two farms with its extra tall chimney folded back over the cylinders. These were in the reverse position on proper traction engines with the flywheel near the front. There was no tender or coal bunker and the fireman had to stand on the ground with water in a tub located where the engine's pump could suck it up to keep the boiler supplied. With fewer moving parts and its high chimney it was much less interesting and in any case boys were not encouraged to enter the yard where it was threshing or sawing up firewood on a whining saw bench with its menacing disc blade.

For me, the so-called Portable engine was scarcely to be compared with a proper traction engine. There was less glamour, because it was so simple, and there was less of the pleasant smell – that combination of steam, coal smoke and hot oil which I later found was relished by almost everyone interested in steam engines of all kinds.

Though less seldom seen there were four other kinds of engines apart from railway locomotives which in those now far off days would excite me. The least rare of these were big ploughing engines, but they worked on the larger fields between villages rather than in the village itself where most of the farmyards were situated. One could hear them as they travelled from one contract to another for they made a different, louder noise than traction engines on the hard road. Hearing a set on the move sometimes prompted me to track them down on my bike, but it was pure luck if I ever saw a pair at work. No matter whether they were ploughing or stirring up stubble with a cultivator or pulling a mole drainer deep in the clay below, they were a splendid sight to behold, standing at opposite ends of the field. Each had an underslung drum winch and, I was told, it held half a mile of shining wire rope, so artfully designed that when winding in the rope packed its coils neatly and tightly on to the drum. With the cable from each engine fixed to the implement, first one then the other pulled it in. The plough had two sets of furrows, one up aloft as the other turned the earth, up to seven furrows at a time, with a gadget which brought down the upper blades for the return to overcome the problem of turning. With the cultivator turning was achieved with a swivel action by its riding man who had to hold on tight over the clods.

Close up of underslung winch on a Fowler ploughing engine.

The ploughing sets were owned by contractors and often worked several miles from base. The crew, usually four men and a lad had their own living van and worked from dawn to dusk on piece-work rates. A rough, tough life – but I've since heard old men who had been operators say, "Ah – those were the days".

Most ploughing engines were built by Fowlers of Leeds and what magnificent machines they were, with two pistons driving a maze of cranks and sprockets. Solidly built and enormously powerful, the largest type weighed just over twenty tons, and could on a wide, clear road, travel at ten miles an hour – much faster than the more usual farm engines.

With the crew on piece work they travelled as fast as their drivers dare from job to job and no wonder the sound could be heard a long way off. Another sound seldom heard on a traction engine was the whistle when at work. It was loud and shrill as it needed to be when coal or water running low was needed. It was the farmers' obligation to keep up these supplies and the whistle blasts were coded to tell which of these essentials was required. Shorter pips were used between the drivers so that each knew when it was his turn to open the regulator for the return haul of the implement. Whilst paying out the wire rope a driver could tend his fire and ensure pressure would rise to the red mark on the gauge for such heavy work, making a barking sound come from the chimney. And as darkness fell, the whistle told the distant driver that the spare helper from the living van had supper ready. A pair of engines could plough up to twenty acres in a day. Working sideways to the cable they had to move on every round or two or the rope would chafe on the engine's road wheels. And the headland beside the hedge or ditch on which they worked had to be left for the farmer to tackle as best he could, since the heavy engines would leave hard wheel marks or ruts to make it a difficult task. A pair of Fowlers are now at rest in the Bressingham Museum.

There was the little haulage engine sometimes to be seen in my boyhood days this too did contract work occasionally for farmers to cart baled hay or straw or gravel, but mostly for granite roadstone for the Council roads. The latter came by rail to Swavesey station and Godfrey's fussy, rattling engine with its canopy roof hauled iron wheeled trucks loaded by hand to be spread on a road. Over this soil was scattered so that as traffic – hooves and wheels – passed over the granites would eventually become bedded down with a flat surface uppermost to form what my father explained was a Macadam road. Godfrey's engine, we were warned, was dangerous. One should never be close to it when it was on the move for one village boy before my time had fallen when in its erratic path and lost his right arm under its wheel. It was not an engine at which one was inclined to stand and stare.

Fairground engines were very different. One came to Over for the annual Feast in September, hauling four or five trailers of equipment. Mannings did not compare with Thurstons which went to towns and the larger villages, but apart from visits when older to Cambridge Midsummer Fair, the Over Feast engine satiated my senses with its subdued splendour. As a toddler the first sight of it had frightened me. The shrouded truck it pulled behind with what looked to me like the barrel of a cannon made me run away for somewhere to hide. I calmed down when told that it was not a cannon but the centre part of the roundabouts with the wooden galloping horses on which to ride to the music of the steam organ. It was almost unbelievable. But that gun barrel next day became the chimney poking out through the top of the Roundabouts with smoke coming out to prove it. And when the promised ride came, what fascinated me was not the up and down motion of the wooden horse on which I was held by the nursemaid, but the little steam engine which drove the set.

This came year after year to Over Feast, and I preferred to stand below and stare rather than ride to see swiftly passing glimpses of it working, performing so much motion at once. The ride was lit by scores of electric lights to show up the brasswork as well as the ornate painting of the set. Electricity was a modern marvel to villagers who had to see by oil lamps and candles and it was the big haulage engine standing in the shadows which produced it from a belt driven dynamo in front of the chimney from the flywheel. That engine and even more the larger and more ornate engines to be seen at Midsummer Fair had for me an aura of mysterious majesty, especially after dark. The driver could scarcely be seen and the moving cranks were hidden by a metal shield. It was very wonderful but very aloof, as if both engine and driver were conscious of their superiority over all other types of road engines.

Once I spoke to the driver, standing far above my head, hoping he might be friendly enough to invite me up beside him. But he did not even answer and with just a supercilious glance as he cracked a large lump of coal told me to clear off. The driver of another type of engine which came to the village every week was more friendly. He drove a steam waggon with the name Foden on the smoke box door in brass and its job was to deliver supplies from St. Ives to the two village shops, one of which was my Father's. But here again the working parts were shielded and only once was I allowed up to see them from above. The engine part of the waggon was so small to have so many moving parts above the boiler barrel, yet in spite of this the driver said it could carry a five ton load at twelve miles an hour because it was high pressured and had a chain drive on to the back axle. In motion it was noisy from the iron shod wheels and the driver admitted that he wished his boss would fit rubber tyres and that it didn't cause horses to shy.

There was also a steam engine stationed in the parish which horses never saw, nor for that matter did I, except on two occasions as a boy. To the west and north the land sloped gently to Over Fen. Its limit was the high bank of the Great Ouse river and beyond was the county of Huntingdon and the Isle of Ely. This area of over 3,000 acres had been subject to flooding until the steam age which allowed it to be successfully farmed. Being well below river level in flood time a steam pump was installed in the 1830's and it was still in use when the occasion demanded to lift water from the fen dykes into the river. It was nearly two miles from the village itself and in wet weather one had to walk down the muddy droves to reach it. But if the engine was working it was worth the effort for inside its house with its landmark chimney was the most amazing piece of steam machinery I'd ever seen. A long low boiler raised steam to make a huge piston push a massive rocking beam up and down quite slowly to turn a flywheel three times the height of a man. Above the cylinder were the spinning balls of the governor. The sight of this was magical, not only with the silent rhythm of the motion, but the smell and the whole atmosphere. From the flywheel a shaft went through the wall to turn a huge, enclosed paddle wheel which lifted the water from the fen dyke into another several feet above which enabled it to run into the wide, swollen river. It was quite close to where the Dutchman Vermuyden made the dead straight New River when he contracted to drain the Fens nearly 300 years before.

Nearly fifty years later, I was resuming aquaintance with various kinds of steam engines which had intrigued me as a boy, one by one examples of them, rusted and derelict arrived at Bressingham to be restored and treasured.

A portable – as it would be towed – with its chimney down. This is a Burrell Compound, believed to be the only one in existence.

At the saw bench with 'Bella', 1947.

'Bella' in trouble in the Fen 1947.

CHAPTER THREE

BRIEF ENCOUNTERS AND A PLUNGE

Steam power in the 1920's was so commonplace that most people believed it would reman so. We were unable to imagine anything else to supersede it, and I for one was too set on my chosen career as a nurseryman to pay much more than a passing interest in the steam engines I happened to see. An engine on the road or on farms aroused a nostalgic affection and the sight of an express train was a thrill. The school train was never exciting unless a 4-4-0 Claud Hamilton replaced the usual 2-4-0 and real interest came with a journey north behind one of the new A 3 Pacifics and an enforced night on York Station was sheer delight. I grew into manhood with no hopes of any wider experiences with steam than any other countryman wedded to the land.

As a young nurseryman with an affection for steam however, there were three occasions when an agricultural engine was used to further my ambitions. By 1931 I had taken over my father's holding at Oakington to which village the family had moved in 1922. A few years later I dug a well and bought a water tower to improve irrigation and having assembled the steelwork and fixed a 1,000 gallon tank on top, the structure had to be raised from the horizontal to the vertical. A friend who owned both traction and ploughing engines for contract work came up with a solution that was obviously better than my intention of jacking the tower up little by little with men on ropes for the final pull.

Harold Papworth was quite confident that with initial jacking and the use of a wire rope and snatch block from one of his engines the tower would be standing above the well in a fraction of the time and cost of jacks and ropes pulled by helpers. Up it went slowly and gently with the engine merely ticking over as its winch drew the rope in. Five years later another larger well had to be dug in a new area to serve the steady expansion of the nursery devoted to perennial plants. At twelve feet deep water began to gush in from the gravel so fast that I could not begin to lay the brick casing on the spokeless wooden cart wheel. Again steam came to the rescue, but the 18 ton Fowler ploughing engine standing above as it sucked water from around me down below was a somewhat fearsome sight. Especially when caving began to make digging dangerous so forcing me to stop and concentrate on laying the bricks.

A third occasion came in 1938. Expansion of the nursery led to renting a derelict orchard – rent free for a year provided I cleared the old apple and plum trees. Again using Harold Papworth's Fowler, with its underslung winch, the trees took less than a week to pull out by the roots. But it took six men most of a month to burn up the brush and pile the trunks and roots to leave the nine acres ready for ploughing. It was then that a neighbour warned us to be careful of any article of clothing being left in the furrow because the land was so hungry that it would be consumed overnight.

In that same year of 1938 I took possession of a badly drained farm in the deep fens at Burwell, hoping to compete with Dutch nurserymen as well as to satisfy a yearning to be a farmer. Dereliction appealed as a reclamation challenge, but when war shattered the nursery business there was no option but to reclaim the Burwell land and switch the Oakington nursery over to food crops. The Burwell farm lay half a mile at the end of a soft, peaty track and when improved drainage allowed deeper ploughing in 1940 dozens of bog oaks were discovered, the notion emerged to lay a narrow gauge railway track using those bog oaks for sleepers. A motor driven sawbench was, however, no match for the incredibly hard bog oak, preserved in the peat for 4,000 years. The circular saw blade protested by becoming blunted and heated enough to make smoke and in the process became so buckled that it refused to cut even when sharpened with a file.

The War ended with over 500 acres of Burwell Fen converted from waterlogged arable and reed or bush covered wilderness to reliable crop producing land, except the part owned by the National Trust as an adjunct to the Wicken Fen Preserve. This was to be allowed to revert to nature and by 1946 I'd given up in favour of a Norfolk farm at Bressingam. It was in the Upper Waveney Valley and it appealed partly because here too was some more or less derelict fenny land offering scope for reclamation.

And early in 1947 during that bitterest of winters a 1912 Burrel Traction engine arrived on a low loader as the fulfilment at last of a longing to be the purposeful owner of a steam engine.

There was work in plenty for it once its requirements were met and the skills needed to drive it were learned. A heavy saw-bench was quickly acquired to reduce a pile of cordwood to fuel logs, but the first day's work left very little with which to keep the home fires burning because *Bella*, the name bestowed on the engine, had used most of the logs in keeping up her fire and steam pressure. It became a pub joke within hours and soon reached the ears of a little man recently retired from business as a steam using timber merchant. Tim Stevens came along and at once went to the cause of the trouble. "Saw blade needs setting", he said, "that's your trouble and I can fix it so it will cut in a couple of hours. The cut needs to be wider and then the blade'll run freer."

It would not have been safe to take the 10 ton engine into the snow covered boggy fen in order to pull up bushes and scrubby trees. And when in mid March the frost at last gave way, heavy rain caused such a flood that the chances of ever doing so appeared to be remote. The spring flood was however followed by a summer drought and when at last the farm crops and nursery plantings were completed Tim Stevens came again having offered to drive *Bella* over a not very safe hump backed brick bridge liable to be risky and on to the unstable fen to be cleared. A few bricks fell into the little river below under *Bella*'s iron wheeled weight but Tim's skill and confidenee was rewarded. For over a month *Bella*'s fires were stoked with waste wood as bit by bit her winch drew out sallow bushes and alder trees. If her wheels sank in now and then in spite of careful prospecting for a dry standing, she could pull herself on to firmer ground by having the wire rope anchored to a sizeable tree or stump. We sweated and unperceived horseflies bit as little by little the clearance expanded. Brushwood fires had to be dug over with ashes still hot to avoid the peaty soil itself burning insidiously downwards. Five weeks work released twelve acres and *Bella*'s cost of £50 for the engine was more than justified.

That first eighteen months at Bressingham had been unexpectedly hampered by frustration and disappointment. Some reluctance on my part to become so deeply involved in the exacting nursery business so decimated by wartime contingencies, had been unsettling. Domestic problems had increased to make emigration to Canada a rosy prospect and leaving a manager in charge we sailed west in September 1948. My three motherless children were joined by a housekeeper and her own fatherless child, but fresh problems arose from the moment we stepped down in Vancouver. The five day journey across Canada behind splendid CPR locomotives was an unforgettable experience but I was not to know that the next 20 months were to be the toughest of my life. Assets dwindled both on Vancouver Island and subsequently in Ontario and when a return to Bressingham became imperative to save what assets remained there, the lesson that escapism never pays off had been well and truly learned. Duly chastened, the financial privations of the two wasted years and the load to be shouldered for years ahead were mitigated by new resolves to restore what had been neglected at Bressingham. To restore the nursery came first; but what angered me most after my unannounced return was the sight of *Bella*'s remains. Only valueless scrap remained for the rest had been cut up by diddicoy dealers who, having promised to pay when they came for the last load, absconded when what was left was not worth collecting, leaving no trace of their whereabouts.

The knowledge of there being no justification to replace the engine for which I had such an affection rankled over the next few years. There was the overriding need to bring the farm up to its full potential and the nursery business back at least to its pre-war status. But gardening trends were against my speciality of Hardy Perennials and Alpines which created the necessity to begin a new concept of how to grow and display them. So began a garden project in 1953 which before it had fully expanded eventually to cover 5 acres was bringing in visitors who unknowingly sparked off the most outlandish of my deviations from the straight professional course a nurseryman is reckoned to take.

It was not the increasing number of visitors on the monthly public openings to the garden which prompted the purchase of another traction engine in 1961. It arose from a parely personal yearning, a sudden release from the self-imposed ban on the grounds that an engine would be a money and time consuming luxury during that eleven year period when both of these were scanty. And it was Flora, my second wife, who pointed out that I needed an entirely different hobby. Gardening was a hobby for many, but not for me. Besides, as a farmer's daughter, Flora too had a nostalgic affection for steam engines, but neither she nor I had visited the rallies of old timers which began in the 1950's and steadily increased as the years passed. For me, the sight of them would have been too much to bear knowing as I did that their value as relics was soaring perhaps beyond my reach. During the early 1950's the scrap dealers were still nosing out and cutting up old farm engines. One heard of some having been sold earlier for as little as £10 each for scrap. I'd seen low loaders carrying them like the knackers of old or ailing horses to end as scrap. But now, in 1961, the new resolve emerged as a spur to act swiftly to replace *Bella* with no thought whatever of going beyond just one as a pet.

First enquiries by telephone led to a visit from a man with a 4 NHP Garrett tractor to sell. I did not take to him. He was obviously a dealer though he said he owned and cared for a fine Showman's Engine. Maybe my estimation of the spirit and purpose of restoring and caring for these noble relics of the Steam Age was unrealistic, for buying and selling them at a profit was in conflict with this notion. "Prices are going up fast", said the man, "this Garrett is just the thing for Rallies – nimble on the roads like, and it'll soon get snapped up if you don't have it – and at £450 it's a bargain". It was a shock rather than a bargain to my way of thinking and he left somewhat disgruntled without making a sale.

A few days later there came a phone call from a parson – the Reverend Stebbing from Tacolneston – whose name had previously been given as a man in the know. I've been scouting around for you, he said, and found someone with a Burrell Single Crank Compound who wants a good home for it. It's well restored and in good order and you can see it if you make an appointment. That appointment was made within minutes and next day we set out for a village near Sudbury.

There she was and under her tilt her deep green paint was clean and her brasswork shiny. "I offered it to a man a month ago", Gerald Dixon the owner explained, "and he said he'd come back to me in a few days but never did. Can you give her a good

Black Prince, *on arrival at Bressingham 1962.*

home? You see, I'm eighty and a bit past taking her out. She's yours for £180 if you're the kind of man I think you are. You're not a dealer, are you?" That assurance was easy to give but the next few days were quite hard to bear for lack of patience. It was hard too to resist the temptation to put her in steam as soon as she arrived, but the March afternoon was too far gone for that. With lingering thoughts of *Bella* I decided to call her *Bertha* out of respect for the departed, and when next day – a Sunday – came, she responded to fire and water as did I to the thrill of seeing her steel rods and red painted crankshaft come to life, turning the flywheel without a sound. It brought a lump to my throat until the need came to remember how to change the road gear and to pull on the fly wheel when cut off steam left the piston rod on top dead centre. There were other things to remember as well. It had taken time to master *Bella* and because engines differ somewhat in temperament, it was said, I'd got to learn how to feel master of *Bertha* also. There were the oiling points not to be overlooked and even more vital to find out the best means of making the waterfeed pump and injector keep the boiler supplied, gauged by the vertical glass tube on the face

Black Prince, *fully restored a year later as a "Showman's".*

plate. There were the cylinder relief valves to open as pressure rose and to keep up the fire with judgement to avoid too much or too little pressure, a factor in which the ash pan flap played a part.

Coal smoke from a steam engine chimney can be an evocative smell, but there was no question of buying coal for *Bertha* any more than there had been for *Bella*. With hundreds of trees on the farm apart from twenty acres of woods no other fuel than what trees needed to be cut could be considered. The saw bench had not been scrapped and having got the hang of driving again by chuntering around the meadow, she was taken to the saw bench where a pile of cordwood had been placed in the spinney. Having alerted Tim Stevens, he was soon on the spot to touch up the circular blade with admiring remarks on what a good engine *Bertha* appeared to be.

He too had once owned a 1909 Burrell Compound with its twin cylinders and because *Bella* had been a single cylinder Tim explained the difference. The smaller cylinder, he explained in his high pitched squeaky voice, is for the live steam direct from the steam chest there on top of the boiler. When the regulator's open the steam from the little one exhausts into the big one beside it at reduced pressure. It's a bigger piston of course – has to be – but it makes a double use of the steam before it goes out up the chimney. But there's only one piston rod going back to the crankshaft, but some engines have two and that's the difference between a double and a single crank compound engine. "Do you follow me?" Even my limited knowledge could follow such an explanation and though I had previously some inkling such an expert as Tim was worth listening to, especially as he was obviously inclined to continue. "The valves which control the entry and outlet of steam to the cylinders work off the crankshaft – but no doubt you know that. What you may not know is it's known as Stephenson's Link Motion and where the valve rods join the crank- shaft they're at an angle to make what we call eccentrics. That's because they work opposite to the motion of the piston – and it wouldn't work at all otherwise, because the valves have to let the steam in and out at the right position of the piston to make it go backards and forrards, d'ye see?" Tim walked round *Bertha* once more, dwarfed by her size, as I waited in case he came out with fresh and helpful information. "She'll make easy work of that wood for logs 'cos that extra cylinder gives her an extra two hoss power. But that's only nominal of course – the official rating. When it comes to real power – especially on that winch with wheels well scotched, she'd pull more than twenty hosses could move if not more. There's nothing to beat steam and seeing one like I used to have makes me wish I'd never parted with her, that it does." My helper at the sawbench was hovering with the big Ballata belt to begin work whilst Tim had his say. Passing one end over the sawbench pulley he handed the other up to me standing on the footplate to loop it over the flywheel. I'd not forgotten the knack of first tying it on with a piece of string and then pulling on the flywheel so that it made full contact with a gentle touch on the throttle as the string was pulled off. "Hah! piped Tim, I bin watching in case you'd forgotten how and now I see you haven't I'll be off. This 'ole gal should give you no trouble but if she does – let me know. I'll soon be here."

The first time or two of having *Bertha* in steam left me with a reluctance to cover her under the canvas tilt until the pressure gauge fell to zero. The warmth and smell and the slow silent motion when standing at the controls was something to be savoured as long as possible, for apart from a day's cutting of firewood there was no excuse for steaming her other than for pleasure – largely confined to myself. But when the first open Sunday for the garden visitors were seen peering under the tilt, the thought came to mind that to have her actively in steam might well prove an added attraction, perhaps giving rides on the bunker to children. This would be much more to my liking than being on call in the garden to answer the questions from visitors or keeping an eye on would-be pilferers. So it proved, but proof that steam nostalgia existed was also evident and with it came another thought, exciting and compelling. If one traction engine was of such interest, an increase in the number of visitors could be expected in relation to the number of engines on display. Out of keeping with a garden maybe, but for a family outing such contrasting variety could well satisfy contrasting interests within a family unit. Gate receipts were being given to charitable causes and more visitors would enable more worth-while donations to be made – and possibly lead to more frequent summer openings. Such thoughts were self propagating, swiftly becoming an impulse to act upon without delay, dispelling all other considerations and possible snags. As a worth-while project the only disability was my scanty bank balance. But the few hundreds there were receipts from writing articles and a book or two and no one could or would dispute my right to spend this as I chose.

More telephone calls led to a visit to a scrap yard in West Norfolk near Stoke Ferry. There were obviously more derelict engines in existence than I'd imagined for here in a field amongst a variety of old farm and building equipment were seven or eight which the owner explained would have been cut up but for the increasing demand for them as relics. "If only I'd ha' known, explained Mr. Palmer. D'you know, I once made up almost a train load for scrap – twenty eight traction engines all in one consignment." Now that scrapping was a thing of the past he was in fact cleaning a pile of old boiler tubes having no scrap value so as to make the engines remaining more saleable. One, a Foster that immediately appealed to me, was in fact already sold to be taken away once retubed.

"That were one of the last Foster's built, it was, and the boiler's as sound as a bell. What about a roller or two – they'd suit you just as well and that set of three over there don't need retubing, 'cos they haint bin here all that long. Came from Dorans the contractors of Thetford, they did."

On being told that I wanted to build up a collection of different types and makes of engines Mr. Palmer looked askance as if I was a somewhat crazy newcomer, he having had a lifetime with engines as a threshing contractor before deciding on hastening the demise of steam as a dealer in scrap. Flora had taken baby Anthea back to the car, the ground between the rows of equipment being too rough to follow where Reg Palmer led me. We came to the three rollers, standing side by side. One had its front end propped up with oil drums because the roll it replaced had been sold separately. This one he explained was a convertible 10 tonner for the roll could be replaced with a wheeled forecarriage to make it of use for haulage if need be. To the question as to whether he had such a unit he shook his head. "You can find a set of drum wheels if you want that one specially. "I'd rather sell the three as they stand – 8, 10 and 12 tonners they are. £200 for the three and a bargain it is. I thought so too but to spend that sum which I'd reckoned on for one traction engine made me wonder how three rollers in need of painting if nothing else could be justified. There had still to be excuses but a choice of rollers for improving farm and nursery roadways could be handy.

They arrived at Bressingham a few days later to stand near *Bertha* but half hidden by a chestnut tree. Saturday came with an urge to put one in steam with no onlookers as the first test of the boiler and tubes was encouragement enough to light the fire. A sudden heatwave had come and sweat ran as the fire waxed fierce with wood smoke belching back as well as going through the tubes to the tall chimney. The needle of the pressure gauge began to lift and two hours from lighting the motion responded to the regulator handle. But more steam was needed before the 12 ton engine could propel itself and I filled the firebox with as much dry wood as it would hold, feeling elated by success so far. Guessing it would be fit to drive in another twenty minutes I went back to the house for a drink, but on returning found the needle on the pressure gauge had already passed the red line at which the safety valve should let out excessive steam. And it was still rising. In sudden fear I set the feed pump going though the boiler was already filled to capacity and then tried to take out some blazing log's with a fire iron. When this effort failed, thoughts of my own safety prompted me to stand behind the other rollers for protection, fearing that an explosion might well occur with safety valve stuck as it was. Half an hour of this anxious vigil was enough to cut me down to size and relief came only when a darting peep revealed a slowly falling needle on the gauge.

I'd been luckier than George Long, my farm foreman, when in 1947 he had undertaken to give *Bella* a wash-out. There were warning plates on most engines that boilers should be emptied and flushed every fourteen days or every hundred working hours. George had come back after tea to find the gauge showing barely five pounds pressure. I advised him to wait a little longer before taking out the mudhole door at the base of the firebox and went off to work with a hoe fifty yards away. Ten minutes later there was a sudden loud roar and a cloud of steam enveloping *Bella*. And then George appeared running as best he could with both hands over the crutch of his trousers and with an expression of agony on his face. The scalding power of even such low pressure steam was enough to lay him up in pain for a fortnight.

By this year of 1961 with expansive ideas of preservation in mind, a renewed respect for steam was timely. Both fire and water were good servants but bad masters, but the lethal power of the two combined was greater perhaps than either, because it was apt to give no warning of explosion. *Bertha* had proved to be safe and sound and children were delighted to be offered a ride sitting up on the logs in the bunker. They queued up as I would have done when young, but soon after the arrival of the rollers a man came up asking to talk privately.

"I've got a Marshall I need to sell quickly," he whispered: "You see, I'm due to get married in a week or two and need the money as well as keeping a promise I made to my intended. It's a double crank eight horse in good nick and I've taken it to rallies with no trouble. Two hundred's all I'm asking for it – but it has to be spot cash."

Holding down renewed excitement, out came the inevitable questions – where it was, and had it a boiler certificate. I studied his expression. It was earnest enough and I sunmed him up as honest. Some chances had to be taken and he did not hesitate long when told that the £200 would be paid if it included delivery from Sleaford. The sight of it when it arrived a few days later was pleasing enough in its deep red paint. But paint had also been used to cover the grime on the wheel hubs and behind the spokes and the lining out was a garish embellishment in an effort to emulate the showman's artistry. But this could be remedied and apart from a thumping noise on the crankshaft the engine itself appeared to be as good as the man said it was.

Within a week or two there came another tip-off from the Reverend Stebbing. He had bought one of a pair of Fowler Ploughing Engines which had been used for a year or two in a chalk pit at Narborough. It was no longer required and the owner was about to sell it for scrap. "I could not bear the thought of that," he confessed, "and I decided to have a go at restoring it myself, though it's the largest model Fowler's built – the AA, and weighs 20 tons. But the reason for telling you is that its sister engine *Bessie* is awaiting the torch in Richard Duce's yard in Cambridge and between us we might save the pair of them."

The motion of a 21 ton Fowler Ploughing Engine from the drivers' standpoint.

The excuse was that the little collection of agricultural engines I had in mind would be very incomplete without a ploughing engine. There it stood in amongst his piles of scrap, huge but forlorn looking after several years of neglect. An attempt to whittle down the asking price failed on the grounds that it would cost Mr Duce time and money to move it to where it could be loaded, hemmed in as it was. And before it was delivered three weeks later my almost one track mind had switched to another relic which also stood out as a necessary addition to the collection. It was a Foden steam lorry – one of the last the Sandbach firm built before switching over to diesel in 1930-31 and two lying derelict in May Gurneys' yard just outside Norwich had been first used as lorries for their public works contracts and then later converted to tarsprayers on the roads. Rust and encrusted tar made them look a sorry sight but although a tèlephone enquiry revealed that they were for sale, they would not name a price after my inspection.

"We'll let you know," the yard manager told me. "The director responsible is away and I'll tell him you want to buy one when he comes in tomorrow – but he might want you to take both."

One alone obviously would be a tough enough task to tackle and there was no telling what condition the little boilers and the intricate moving parts were in. Both tar tanks had been removed and in any case a lorry buck would have to be made or found to restore it to the original. And one had no chimney. Yet patience was again hard to find as I waited for the director's call, to the extent of losing sleep at night, and after three blank days I could stand it no longer and asked for him over the phone. Quite curtly came his answer. "Whoever told you they were for sale should have known better. They were sold to Mr. George Cushing over a year ago and he's still not taken them away, but he's promised to do so right away."

With slumping spirits I fretted. George Cushing's reputation of having a yard full of engines already at Thursford and of his having beautifully restored a few including a Showmans, was widespread. It was also said that he was anything but a dealer and would never part with anything he had acquired over the years. But it was worth a try and the best approach would be a letter, carefully worded. To my surprizse and delight it worked, for having read it he must have been touched to telephone suggesting a visit in order to make a choice since he only needed to keep one.

It was the arrival of the Foden at about the same time as the Fowler Plougher that inklings came from my family of my being obsessed, or of having taken leave of my senses. It was as much from what was unspoken as queries on how to cope with such obvious dereliction, the cost of which might have been better spent on more deserving causes nearer home. Previous excuses on my part were no longer valid or seen as reasonable. From intending to possess only one, a few months ago, there were now seven mostly hulks, cluttering up the yard near the house. Tolerance had been shown but it was to be stretched and diminished still more when yet another offer came. This was from the owner of a Foster single cylinder traction engine in Lincolnshire who phoned me to say that he'd decided to sell. He'd fulfilled an ambition to buy a Sentinel lorry and could not afford to run both. He had taken the Foster to rallies but wanted something much more speedy on the roads than a 5 m.p.h. Traction engine. At £200 it was clearly a bargain and if I had to run my bank account a bit into the red it was surely no disgrace, and only the bank need know. And what was more, it would be such a treat to see it at work threshing a stack of wheat, harvested the old fashioned way at my behest with a binder. The excuse for this had been to have thatching straw for sale now that combines had come to make such straw almost unavailable. The underlying reasons however were to fulfil my long standing ambition to thresh out my own, corn with my own engine even if the threshing drum and elevator had to be hired.

So ended an eventful year. It had begun with only wistful hopes of owning a replacement for *Bella*. Just one, for old times sake, and to savour steam now and then. And now there were nine because in between the Foden and the Foster I'd accepted the offer of a rare Burrell Portable not far away for under £100. True it was not self propelled and needed a powerful tractor to move it. But since such engines were the fore-runners of the agricultural tractors and were in use for a century or more, then it was needed to complete the collection even if at the back of my mind there was a reservation that 1962 might see one or two more somewhere to make the colleotion more complete. And if amongst my excuses there was the repeated belief of these old engines proving to be a good investment as values rose from nostalgia and scarcity, I knew I would be as reluctant as George Cushing to part with any.

Jack Clements and the author on the Marshall after restoration, 1962.

CHAPTER FOUR

A PRIDE OF ENGINES FOR THE MAVERICK

It has been said that whatever generates a mere fascination for steam in the human breast, true enginemen like poets and artists are born with something extra in their blood, Since nostalgia for steam took a hold on so many, a few such were lucky enough to acquire an engine as a hobby, They may believe fervently they have the ability to bring it back to life and gain enormous pleasure in mastering its intracacies as a driver. But they would probably be very conscious of not being true enginemen of long standing and to yearn for the help and advice of someone who was. Such a man was Roger Garnham who in fact called in one day on chance to ask if I needed help and advice, I'd never met or heard of him before but he explained that he had always worked with steam engines and was still using a steam roller for his road contractor employer at East Dereham, If retubing was needed he would gladly come in the evenings or at weekends. There was nothing about him I could not take to – and his very unassuming approach appealed, he remarked with a wry smile that his smallness of stature was an advantage when, working in cramped spaces such as an engine firebox.

Novice that I was, the most effective means of testing for rusty, leaky tubes was to fill up the boilers of the most likely runable engines with water and raise steam, But having told Roger of my recent experience when the safety valve failed, I learned from him that leaky tubes readily show up with unheated water in the boiler. After a few helpful visits Roger remarked that he knew the very man to come and work more or less full time. "He's not so much a boiler man, but what he don't know about the mechanical side isn't worth knowing. He's close to seventy, but still agile as a monkey."

Jack Clements turned up on a racing bike one Saturday morning. Lean and wiry, wearing an old trilby hat, he walked around each engine as if they were old familiars, saying very little. "I'm in a job," he muttered, "but not with steam and if you want me to come I'll chuck it in for half a crown an hour if that'll suit you. I never thought I'd get the chance of working on steam again. And if you're short off tules I've got me own I can bring."

Tools were in fact as inadequate for the tasks ahead as was the building which would have to serve as a workshop. Apart from an old high roofed barn in which men had once threshed out grain with flails but which now housed a few implements and pig feed, there was a lean-to pigsty outside backing on to walls on two sides. Jack said it would do if the three empty sows could go elsewhere. Since it was summertime and with the necessary eviction made, the Marshall was driven in. He listened intently to the thumping noise on the crankshaft and was soon at work with his spanners on what he said was a loose bearing. He had noticed other minor defects which took a week to remedy, whilst I scraped the wheel spokes which had been daubed to cover grime and rust down to bare metal for a proper repaint. From the first day Jack was very emphatic on how work should be done. "Skimp a job," he said, "and it'll like as not want doing again. I served my time as an apprentice mechanic and it taught me a lesson I've never forgot when the boss made me do a job I'd skimped all over again – in me own time. Paint work wern't my job, but I found out that you got to get down to bare metal if its old paint or rust and then give it a coat of red lead. No primer to come up to red lead there een't."

Jack came out with one tale after another about old time working conditions and the tricky jobs he'd done. He'd worked for many years at a foundry and steam engine concern in Diss, eventually becoming a journeyman trouble shooter and fitter for the firm's widespread customers till it became obvious that he was the foremost steam expert for miles around. I was lucky to secure his services, especially at his age.

Work on the Marshall was thereabouts completed when the big Fowler came in on a low loader. I volunteered to steer it when released from the platform, the slope down to be checked by a winch on the lorry. It was tricky because the engine wheels were so wide apart that they were very near the edge of the platform. Beginning on a tightened, checking wire rope, it suddenly slackened as the lorry driver let gravity take over and with no applicable brake on the engine down it went onto the ground with a rush, with one wheel crashing over the side regardless of my frantic attempts of correction on the steering wheel. When the 22 ton engine came to rest well clear of the loader, Jack swore at the driver.

"Blast it man! – you shouldn't have let her go like that. You might have known it would be out of control and could do a hell of a lot of damage."

To me he muttered that it was a mercy I wasn't thrown off, standing as I was with nothing to hold on to but the steering wheel which the sudden jerk had made spin violently out of my hands. But no damage had been done and awkwardly placed as it was, a test came for the Marshall to move it away on to the nearby meadow. Later, Jack saw no harm in steaming it, provided cold water revealed no leaky tubes. They held and with the fire well alight, the pressure gauge needle began to lift, but no movement came from the working parts when the regulator was opened. Nor could either muscles or levers make the flywheel budge to get the motion going. Jack said more pressure might help. Sooner or later it had to be set in motion or he would not know whether any repairs or adjustments were needed. But not even 100 lb. pressure had any effect and four of us with levers against the flywheel spokes made no difference.

Jack chuckled as he suggested lighting up the big Burrell Portable which had arrived only the day before. "Let's steam test that an'all and put the big drum belt over both engine flywheels. If that don't shift it then nothing won't." Two hours later, with the regulators of both engines open, the belt slipped a little over the Fowler's flywheel and then slowly and gradually the wheel, along with the motion began to move as both engines were throttled down. And within minutes the Fowler was ticking over without a sound, the pistons and valve rods sliding in and out with fascinating rhythm: "Quieter than a sewing machine and not a thing wrong as I can see," Jack commented as if it was the result he'd expected all along.

It was Jack who went with me to inspect the two Fodens, now transferred to Thursford. George Cushing repeated his offer to make a choice and Jack was soon crawling over and under the working end, under its wooden cab where a driver could but sit

'A Tug of War' with the "Garrett" 4 h.p. Tractor.

down with very little room for his knees and feet. He turned the little flywheel to study the motion and tapped the firebox from below to check any weakness by the sound of metal against metal. After half an hour he said he reckoned the one without a chimney was the best and in settling up the modest sum George Cushing asked – "Just enough to cover transport from Norwich", he then added, "I'm glad you're having it,though I don't reckon to sell to anybody. That dealer feller from down your way has been plagueing me for it – you know who I mean – and when I told him I'd given you first refusal, he said 'He's only a flower grower and no engineman'. But I reckon you'll make a good job of it now I know you're not a dealer and got a man like Jack Clements there to help."

All very encouraging, but on the way home Jack hesitatingly said he'd need help from me in the shape of a more weather-proof building in which to work. It was a top priority as I well knew, but I did not know that Jack's skill included erecting buildings. The old barn faced east with ill fitting doors high enough to take loads of sheaves inside. The space between this and stables and outhouses opposite had been an open yard for wintering store cattle. Scouting around, old tramway standards and telegraph poles were obtained for stanchions, second-hand timbers for rafters and asbestos sheets for the roof, and by the time autumn gales and rains came the yard was covered. And so were most of the engines. The big Fowler was driven into the old barn and the Foden in the most convenient place for Jack with light coming from a large window bought earlier from a now demolished school.

The first task was to remove the hind wheels from the Fowler so as to get to the otherwise inaccessible parts for scraping down and painting, as well as the reverse side of the wheels. These, a good six feet tall with iron tyres nearly two feet wide, weighing close to a ton each, appeared to be a formidable operation, but Jack knew exactly how to draw them away from the heavy steel axle. Jacking up the main body to rest on wood blocks so that the wheels just cleared the floor, he grimly remarked that if a loosened wheel fell over on to anyone it would maim them for life – if they survived at all. With crowbars, we began to wriggle the suspended wheel. The engine's weight had already broken through a thin cement surface to make clearance more difficult, but fraction by fraction it was eased off until it stood clear, scotched and propped. With a nonchalant, "That's that – now let's have the other one" Jack rolled a cigarette and grinned when I said it had not taken so long as I'd expected: "You've gotta know what to expect with such jobs. I've taken wheels off in me time alone, but it's better with two, even if one of them has to be told what to do."

The next vital task towards full restoration of the Fowler was to test the soundness of the firebox. It had stood up to being steamed with no more pressure than it took to move itself, but as Jack explained now was the time to find out if it was safe to work at at its full pressure of 180 p.s.i. Neglect of regular washouts and accumulations of shale and mud in the shelled water spaces could spoil a box long before its time, Jack said. "I've known 'em to bulge and crack – and go off like a cannon". With the ashpan and firebars removed, he crawled under with a lantern into the dark iron cavern, having told me to hold a hammer against the first in the many rows of stay heads. These stay bolts, dozens of them on all sides of the firebox, were to hold the inner and outer shell of the box securely. They were rivetted to be watertight on either side of the water space of about 4 inches. As I struck each stay bolt head from the outside, Jack could feel the impact on the hammer he held against the opposing head on the inside and know from this whether or not the bolt was sound. Any lack of concussion would reveal a weakness or complete wastage, but all appeared to be sound. He then tapped all other areas to judge the thickness of the steel plate by the sound.

"I'd say it's sound enough for what we want," he said as he crawled back. "Not too bad at all, considering, but do you ask Roger to take a look at it when he comes next. He's more of a boiler man than me but though I'm a mechanic by trade, I got roped in for all sorts of engine repairs in me time."

With two such experts there were hopes that all the engines would be steamable once the less vital repairs had been accomplished. Jack decided to dismantle the working parts on the Foden and renew some of the worn bearings. This might well take a few weeks working alone, but as he rermarked it was likely to take a few months to scrape down and repaint both the Foden chassis and the main body of the Fowler. And for this tedious work three more volunteers had come forward. The first was a

The Foden Steam Wagon, 1930 with solid tyres.

long service gardener, Percy Piper, followed by Ben Francis the pigman and then by a young gardener Dennis Leeper. For them, at work on farm and nursery by day, it was in the evenings when mostly there were four of us at work. We used wire brushes, paint scrapers, flat file ends with paraffin to loosen encrustations of grease and tar caked grime. In the high old barn it was too dark to work even in daylight without some artificial light on parts to be scraped and chiselled down to bare shining metal. The big window was helpful to Percy who first attacked the tar caked Foden in the newly roofed part, but the whole place was draughty. Percy and Ben rigged up a screen over the doorless side open to the easterly winds with cut-up fertiliser bags and pieces of old canvas tilts. There was no heating at all and no overhead lights so that only the dim glow revealed our whereabouts after dark from the one spotlight, the hurricane oil lamp and the candles which one or two of us had to use.

Making do had always been a failing of mine and though it may have been of some encouragement to those who worked together with me on such tedious jobs, with hindsight I marvel that they did so at the time. There was no reward other than beer or coffee which Flora, pityingly, brought out to us most evenings. Each of us worked alone, each with his own light such as it was. To move from one place to another meant taking the light as well to other engines stored under the same roof for winter. And an evening's work often achieved no more than two feet or so of ironwork, or two or three spokes on a wheel scraped down to the bare metal.

When spring came in 1962 both engines were well on the way to being restored, with working parts overhauled by Jack and painting begun. For some of us the mass of our legitimite business had to come first but I would often sneak an hour or two for painting. Red lead came first. This showed up any unevenness in the metal caused by rust and where so pitted, filler had to be scraped in to make a smooth surface to take a grey primer. Then came the two undercoats, followed by two top coats of paint and sometimes three, before the final varnish brought up the gloss. Between each coat of paint wet and dry emery paper was rubbed over the whole surface to achieve the best possible finish. The contrast once this stage was reached brought feelings of pride in a long, tedious job well done. But the peak of triumph and the test of achievement could only come when, at last, a fire could be lit to produce steam under pressure enough to bring a noble old timer back to active life.

Two lucky finds brought the Foden nearer to completion. An ex- railway delivery lorry to be scrapped had a buck which as near as dammit fitted the chassis exactly to bring the whole back to its original appearance. And a genuine chimney was found in Thetford. Roger, having driven this type of vehicle before was the first to drive what we named *Boadicea*, its mechanism and controls being too complicated for me. Unlike traction engines which were steered by means of chains on the front axle activated by a worm gear, it had Ackermann steering not unlike that of a modern lorry. The chain drive to the rear axle could produce a top speed of 18 m.p.h. and all four tyres were of solid rubber – amongst the last to be fitted before legislation against solid tyres put an end to their use on the roads. A loophole in the law, however, enabled *Boadicea* to be licensed as a tractor at only £2 in view of the little mileage it would ever do as a preserved steamer.

A much greater thrill came on the day when *Bessie* the Fowler ploughing engine was ready to be steamed. The fire had to be lit and stoked where it had stood in the barn to save the cost of steaming Bertha or Brenda to haul her out into the open for lighting up. It was Easter Monday and for once the needs of the garden and nursery took second place. With steam up, Flora holding year old Anthea in her arms and Bridget, my eldest daughter watching, I backed *Bessie* out away from the murky old barn into the yard. They joined me on the footplate for a sedate ride round the other farm buildings to watch the working parts running so smoothly from above. Virtually the only noise came from the grinding of iron wheels on the gravelled roadway and at this moment came a rich reward for labours past. "Perhaps you're not so crazy as I'd been thinking after all," was Bridget's comment.

Spring, as always, made its well-nigh total demand on the time available. For a nurseryman with a five-acre garden to look after as well, April and May were crucial months. But with the approach of Whitsun I began to look forward more and more to the adventure I felt sure it would be to drive *Bessie* to the annual Woodton Rally on Whit Monday. Mr Stebbing had volunteered to drive since he had Cissie half stripped for restoration, so *Bessie* would be the only ploughing engine there. She looked smart enough we thought, to gain the prize for the best engine in the parade, but we must allow ample time for the journey of twenty six miles.

These big Fowlers are not the easiest engines to steer, and as I was of much more robust physique than the Rector, I took my stance on the steering wheel, with legs astride the tender for balance. There was no question of sitting down and it was soon evident that muscle; alertness and judgement would all be needed. It was at nine o'clock on the Whit Saturday that we edged out on to the main road. Despite holiday traffic on roads leading eastwards to the coast, the police had advised me not to take the risks attendant on taking such a wide vehicle on to by-roads. The first of my worries were 'cats eyes'. The engine was too wide to keep between them and the curb or grass verge. In places I could not prevent the off-side wheels running over them, since to straddle them gave oncoming traffic too little room to pass. If I tried to keep *Bessie* close enough to the verge to avoid them, the near-side front wheel was just as likely to mount the verge, and if it did so no power that I could exert on the steering wheel would guide her back on to the road again. She would simply draw farther still off the road, and only by stopping and reversing could I bring her back. Maybe the steering chains were a bit slack. Maybe I lacked experience as a steersman, but since the slightest alteration in direction meant turning the handle several times, it was small wonder that to keep exactly on the foot or so next to the verge was almost impossible.

Beyond Victoria Road railway bridge, Jack Clements was waiting for us, as he had said he would be. It had taken nearly an hour to travel that three miles in spite of the fact that flat out, *Bessie* could do ten or twelve miles an hour in top gear. The Rector had already reported that one of the two injectors would not work. Jack said that was one thing he had not felt very happy about, and because of his general anxiety he had decided to come too. "Wait a minute while I get my old bike," he said, running smartly down the path to his nearby house. He was back, wheeling his old racing bike before I could explain that he had no need to bring it. "No," said Jack, "I'll ride me 'ole bike – it'll be handier if there's any trouble."

For the next few miles, crossing the main road at Scole and taking the east coast route to Harleston, there was no trouble, at least not as far as the engine itself was concerned. Jack on his bike was rather like a shepherd dog, sometimes in front, sometimes beside *Bessie*, but always on the alert for trouble. Every now and then we had to stop to back off the verge which I'd allowed *Bessie* to mount in my anxiety to allow cars enough room to pass: Sometimes when a queue of cars was building up behind we pulled in to let them through. I'd stopped worrying about smashing 'cats eyes', after checking that the first few we'd run over appeared undamaged by *Bessie*'s great iron wheels.

"We ought to stop for water at Harleston," the Rector shouted. You had to shout to be heard above the clatter. The first big garage in Harleston was owned by Cecil Knights, the Norfolk Steam Engine Club's secretary and his brother, and it seemed the obvious place to stop to fill up *Bessie*'s tank from the supply they were sure to have. But Cecil was not there, having gone to Woodton with his own Garrett engine. His brother came out and said it would be better if we took a side road where water could be had without hindrance to the traffic now thickening fast, since the tank might take half an hour to fill. "But it means backing and turning round to get there," he said, and he added a warning to avoid running over the iron inspection lids over the underground petrol tanks supplying the range of pumps. "How's the water?" Jack Clements called up to the Rector. "Pretty low," was the Rector's reply as he pulled back the reversing lever, while I slewed round the front wheels.

The road was narrow and the slope up which we had to back was steep. The traffic was bothersome, and one shunt was not enough, with these petrol tank covers to be avoided. These factors, as well as the noise, made co-ordination between driver and steersman difficult, and when *Bessie* ran down forwards from the slope for the second shunt, it was too fast for me to get the needful turns on the steering wheel. It was too fast for the narrow space as well, and one front wheel caught the opposite curb with a thwack which made *Bessie* shudder. It made me shudder too, when I found the steering jammed as a result. "Back right up this time," I shouted. We were blocking the road completely at right-angles, and nothing short of backing into the yard of the garage could save the situation, since the steering must be freed before anything else. Already I was feeling aggrieved because all this trouble would have been saved had we not been asked to turn to go elsewhere for water.

In this present position I noticed that we would be well clear of the petrol tank lids, and once up the slope and on the level again the tank could be filled just the same. But our troubles here were not ended. They had in fact only just begun because as *Bessie*'s front wheels left the road, allowing the piled-up traffic to move once more, there came a sudden roar and a gush of steam through the firehole door, which shrouded *Bessie* instantly. The Rector and I left our places rather hurriedly, but Jack was the first man I met through the cloud of steam. "Fusible plug," he announced bluntly. "Stands to reason – short of water, back up the slope – head down, no water over the crown of the firebox – fusible plug blows – simple as that. That's what fusible plugs are for, but it shouldn't have happened none the more for that."

The Rector had little to say. As driver his was the onus, and perhaps the shame of having 'dropped a plug', since for old enginemen this occurrence is a reflection upon skill, and under no avoidable circumstances should a driver take such a risk when the water level reading is low. But these circumstances were unexpectedly difficult, and it was not for me to blame him. Nor could I blame him for allowing *Bessie* to run forward so fast as to hit the opposite curb, because there was excuse enough for getting flustered with so much fuss and bother.

With the lead-filled core of the fusible plug melted, the hole allowed all the steam in the boiler to squirt downwards on to the fire. The fire was quenched long before all that steam had spent itself, but by the time we ourselves had swallowed some much needed drink, Jack had gone to work on the steering. The worm gear was jammed, but in half an hour Jack had freed it. "Let's have a bite to eat now," he suggested. "We've got to wait till she cools down enough for me to get that fusible plug out."

It was of course the only way to get on the move again. The plug must be unscrewed and refilled with molten lead, and not until it was replaced could the boiler be filled again, and the fire re-lit. I had reckoned on being the one to crawl under the engine to remove the heavy ashpan and firebars, so as to get at the plug, since there was no other way of doing it. No one else could be expected to do what was bound to be a very sweaty, dirty job. But I hadn't reckoned with Jack either, for though he had turned seventy he could be very determined, and he had made up his mind it was his job. After we had eaten our lunch sandwiches Jack said it would be cool enough to begin. The ashpan was dropped and pulled clear; one by one the still hot firebars were hauled out, each one making us splutter with ash dust. An hour later the plug was unscrewed. One of the garage men melted some lead in a crucible and filled up the hole. By three o'clock the fire was lit once more, and by half past four we were again on our way to Woodton, with Jack back on his bike as shepherd. The injectors were still giving trouble, and several stops were made while Jack tapped and fiddled with them. They seemed to take it in turns to fail, but what we dreaded was that both should refuse to work. Beyond Homersfield we stopped at the 'Dove' Inn for tea, and were allowed to drain a handy water butt to replenish the tanks.

Flora arrived in the car, saying she had found it easy enough to follow our trail of wheel and water marks. On again, we were soon able to turn off the still busy main road, and headed towards Earsham. *Bessie*'s speed had increased, since now the road was mostly ours. But hopes of reaching Woodton that day faded. With four miles still to go I was given permission to pull into a farm yard as dusk was falling. With Flora and the car still in attendance it was the sensible thing to do, and though we did not care to admit it, Jack, the Rector and I had had enough for one day.

It was not until early on Whit Monday morning that *Bessie* finished the journey. Once on the big meadow at Woodton Old Hall, with thirty other engines already there, we began furiously to clean off the dust which by now had dimmed *Bessie*'s shining paint. The judge came round. "What a pity you painted her blue. Fowlers should always be either black or brown – didn't you know that?" was the muttered comment. When the prize winners were announced, *Bessie* was not among them, though it was whispered that but for the colour she would have gained the rosette for the smartest engine there.

Next day, with Jack driving and me again at the wheel, we took the by-roads back to Bressingham. Jack did not reckon to be an engine driver, but if he saw a pond or a ditch, or any sign of water, he'd stop and say, "Let's top the tank up – there's no telling when we shall find any more. I don't want that plug to drop with me. I'd never live that down."

To meet the increasing influx of visitors monthly openings had given way to fortnightly by 1961. But this quickly proved to be unsatisfactory and in 1962 it was every Sunday afternoon from the first Sunday in June. Although a BBC Gardening programme had boosted visitors it was quite evident now that the engines were a major additional attraction; especially if one or two were in steam. And the popularity of free rides on the bunker was sometimes embarrassing, pleasure though it was for me. There was always the risk of a youngster falling off the uneven perch on logs of wood and the increasing number of visitors made less of the car park on which to drive.

Far from eight engines being a sufficient collection to meet the obvious nostalgic public interest, it set off my collecting urge again, once *Bessie* and *Boadicea* had been fully restored. The latter, as a steam lorry, had stood for a time as the ultimate ambition. But once it became owned and restored my mind began to veer towards other distinctive types of road using engines without which the collection would still be sadly lacking in completeness. No tractor type, like the Garrett offered by the dealer was represented, but this was remedied by yet another unexpected offer. And it was indeed a little Garrett. Its owner had lost interest in taking it to Rallies and he saw no point in keeping it locked in a shed where no one could see it. The price was well above what others had cost, but still less than that asked by the dealer over a year before. It had a canopy and on the side of the boiler barrel of faded brown paint was the original Garrett trade crest, indicating its date of 1924. In action it was a tricky little machine to drive with a regulator so sensitive that movement of the lever of less than half an inch would vary the speed from racing at six or seven miles an hour to slack off to no motion at all.

One or two well wishing visitors had suggested that a Showmans road locomotive would be a great attraction. At first this prospect had no great appeal because it would be somewhat out of keeping with the rest. But at heart I knew this to be a sour grape attitude and the main reason for dismissing the idea had been on the score of cost. Showmen's engines splendidly adorned with twisted brass rods and with paintwork as ornate as could possibly be were at the top of the market, and in good condition worth five to ten times as much as an ordinary traction engine. To purchase one such was way beyond my means, but a thought came to nag consistently that somewhere there might be a low priced one still lying derelict somewhere. That George Cushing had at least two, as yet unrestored, was well known, but it was unlikely in the extreme he'd part with one of them.

"I'd not thought of parting", came his answer over the phone, "but you're welcome to come and have a look." A glimmer of hope for what had now suddenly become almost as great an obsession as was the Foden the year before came over me. George showed us two in an out of the way yard lying very derelict indeed. He explained that he still hoped and intended to restore them as he'd done so splendidly with '*Victory*', having bought all four of the Thurstons fleet of Burrell's Showmans when auctioned years before. "I'll tell you what I'll do," he said finally. "I'll help you to locate one elsewhere if I can, being a bit in the know like, and if I can I'll go with you to inspect it and if nothing turns up then I'll see if I can't let you have one of these – 'cos you made a rare good job of that Foden in a lot less time than I'd have thought you would. But there, you've got a couple of good'uns in old Jack and Roger to help you."

A few weeks later George telephoned one evening to say that he'd located a derelict Burrell Showman's in a yard near Tring and would be arriving at Bressingham at ten next morning if that suited. It did, but it was past midday before he turned up and mid-afternoon before we were inspecting what had been 'Black Prince'. It was an engine with a past for since 1904 it had been used for haulage and later converted to a Showman's for Grays of Hampstead Heath fame. During the war it had been used for pulling down dangerous buildings following air raids on London; and since then it had lain discarded in breakers' yards at Twyford and Ewell. Mr Evans the owner was a scrap merchant, but it seemed he was alive to the reawakened interest in steam.

Scrapyards, I was finding, were depressing places to visit. So much junk littered the ground. One had to try and be as hard-headed as the owners of such yards; not like my type which easily betrays to an experienced dealer whether or not an article is really wanted. A shrewd dealer sums us up and is liable to fix his price accordingly. But here time was running out and I was a hundred miles from home. George poked, peered and tapped and finally told me enough to do a deal with the owner which concluded with a cheque for under £300. "If you don't hit any snags I've not seen," George whispered, "it'll be worth ten times what you've paid for it when its restored."

But when it arrived at Bressingham the look on people's faces was one of incredulity. "A load of scrap" was heard from one man, and for weeks uncomplimentary mutterings were reported to me which made me wish it could have been stowed away out of sight. When space was made, it was, but not for shame but because Jack, undaunted as always, was ready to make room for it the cramped make-shift workshop. Patiently, almost lovingly, he took off every part of the motion from pistons to crankshaft using tripod sheerlegs he'd made up for the heavier items. Safety valves, controls and gear sprockets and flywheel followed and then all the wheels and steering gear. He examined the firebox minutely testing the stays by tapping and marking with chalk wherever a different hammer sound revealed a suspected fault or weakness, whilst Roger and I knocked out the boiler tubes – all 60 of them, wasted as they were. But at least the all important firebox was reasonably sound and all the stay bolts responded to the double hammer test. A few weak spots in the inner shellplate would need to be thickened by welding and the general condition was good enough to set about not only the scraping and painting but to find a supply of solid rubber for the tyres, material for the canopy and twisted brass for its uprights, as well as a dynamo. As a Showman, the latter was essential for making electric light and a metal platform projected over the smoke box and beyond the chimney was fitted for that purpose. Burrells of Thetford had produced at least two types of Fairground engines and *Black Prince*, built in 1904, had a shorter wheelbase than some of the later models with a slightly longer boiler, often with a crane fitted on the coal bunker behind. But both types had a higher bunker and were more capacious than other traction engines to hold more coal on top and more water in the tank under the footplate. Another feature was the belly tank underslung to the boiler barrel, enabling less frequent stops for water on long journeys, and it had a solid, unspoked flywheel as well as springs.

A well wisher had presented us with an old lathe which pleased Jack greatly. It was the first machine tool to be installed apart from a small pillar drill and a bench grinder. On these, Jack's old but capable hands refurbished metal wherever required, whilst Percy, Ben and I in the evenings scraped away at the bodywork. As autumn came it was some relief to get stuck into what we all knew would be a pretty formidable job and I was still smarting from an incident which was somewhat to my discredit and shame.

The Marshall had come in for a more thorough overhaul and repaint to its original deep red and Jack had, he believed, cured the thumping noise on the crankshaft. Roger had recommended a complete retubing as well, but to save time and money I'd agreed to only a few to be replaced. Having entered it for a big Rally to be held in Lord Townshend's grounds at Raynham forty miles away, it was despatched there in a contractor's low loader in advance. A feeling of considerable pride was mine as I took off the tilt in the early morning of the first Raynham Day which had been organised and publicised by Dick Joice of Anglia Television. Other engines and owners were there in the assembly yard, all agog with the prospects of a very large crowd of onlookers and a fine day – none more so than me. In between tending the fire, *Beatrice* was oiled and cleaned to become an object of pride, but just as the great moment came to drive her the mile or so to the venue park, a gush of steam came out of the chimney and through the firehole door. A boiler tube had blown and thinking back to Roger's ignored advice, the day's prospects were shattered for me. Shame and sorrow were such that I could have wept and though I accepted another owner's offer to be dragged to the Park, a part of me would have preferred to leave *Beatrice* there and go home to work off my chagrin with a hoe as I'd often done before to relieve my feelings.

Work on *Black Prince* became difficult with the onset of the most severe winter since 1947. Percy patched up his meal-sack screens but still the bitter east winds forced a way in, and an old upright stove served only to warm hands when cold made them too numbed to use a tool. Water pipes, eighteen inches below ground froze up, for unlike 1947 there was no snow to prevent frost penetration. On the nursery and farm jobs became hard to find and to avoid standing off some staff two or three were drafted in to scrape down two of the Burrell Rollers. These were the eight and twelve tonners, for the 10 ton convertible had gone. A visitor had coveted it and seeing no future for it as part of the collection – being neither roll or traction – I let it go at a modest profit. Nothing had been done to the other two mechanically and boiler wise they were in fair condition, needing only the tedious job of scraping down to be painted when warmer weather came.

It did not begin till mid March, and if the long hard frost had killed thousands of plants in the nursery and made spring land work late, it had at least enabled *Black Prince* to be much nearer to complete restoration than would otherwise have been the case. By the time several applications of filler paste had rendered pitted surfaces smooth and a total of eleven coats of paint had been applied, it was again worthy of its name. And when Bob Rolph our local expert had lined it out and cleverly inscribed my name along the valance of the canopy – for love rather than for money – pride of ownership had to be nursed quietly rather than expressed. With new rubber tyres fixed the engine was drawn out into the open yard and the fire lit – for the first time in over twenty years. The anxieties, the hard graft and the cold were now of no account. And when with enough steam to make the piston work, it was sheer joy to behold. Jack had made a splendid job of setting the valves as with all else he'd undertaken. And if he was not so happy with the wear in the gear sprockets which were impossible to make good, there was no doubt about its being entered for the Woodton Rally at Whitsun. As with *Bessie*, a steersman as well as driver were needed for a journey and Roger was obviously the one for the latter, with me again as steersman. Sprung hind wheels as well as rubber tyres made this journey vastly easier than on *Bessie* the year before. This time there was no doubt in the judges' minds on which was the best restored engine, gaining as it did the annual premier prize.

The excuse of buying just one more relic to complete the collection had worn too thin to repeat by the year 1963. There was no point, therefore, in using it when news came on the grapevine that a Sentinel Timber Tractor was for sale near Oxford. With a need to visit a nursery as a lame excuse, Flora, Anthea and Jenny, our second newly arrived daughter, joined me for the ride. Jack Wharton – a pioneer in the engine restoration field, explained that the Sentinel was for sale only because he had embarked on restoring to perfection a hulk of 1880. The Sentinel was 50 years its junior and on pneumatic tyres. It was, Mr Wharton believed, the only one left of the twelve this once famous firm made for timber work. It had two engines; one for propulsion and the other to work a winch, able to draw in tree trunks and load them on to a drug for transport. Though of short wheel base, it was quite massive weighing 11½ tons and the vertical tub-like boiler was pressured to over 500 psi. When new it had cost the then steep price of £2,500.

The boiler had been taken out for inspection, but having passed it was a bargain at £350 – or so I thought. Subsequently Jack Clements and I had to spend many hours with pulley blocks to entice the scores of studs in one section to sink neatly in their opposite holes in the other. After that. time-taking effort, all went well and it was pleasing to note that my eldest son Robert was showing more interest in it than any other of the engines. He was more mechanically minded than his younger brother Adrian and although I fancied he found other engines somewhat slow and ponderous, the Sentinel was so different to them and was capable of 35 mph. Roger too had driven an even more speedy Sentinel in his time at fifty miles an hour with a 6 ton load. Quite happily Robert undertook to paint it and when resplendent in blue and white, he and Roger drove out of the gate on a test run. Very little smoke came from the chimney which barely cleared the driving cab and no puffing from the exhaust beyond a whispered 'push-push'.

Roger had known for some months that if he decided to leave his Dereham employer there would be plenty of work for the rest of his life at Bressingham. It was good to hear him say this was what he wished to do, in October 1963. He and Jack made an excellent pair, each specialists in their own field of boilersmith and fitter and they worked together as a pair of highly skilled men, dedicated above all to steam. If enthusiasm and drive were my main attributes, theirs was the vital skill and knowledge, deserving of the greatest respect and encouragement. Others, such as Percy and Ben were still part-time volunteers and it pricked my conscience to see them at work on the less skilled but tedious tasks when I could not join them, though I'm quite sure they understood that I had duties as the boss liable to prevent participation. When working within hearing distance of Roger and Jack, it was worth listening not only to what they said, but how they addressed themselves to the task. Often it was as if an engine, in part or as a whole, was alive and they were as surgeons discussing a biopsy or a prognosis. And if I asked them to explain once they'd come to a decision or achieved some good result Jack would spread a grin over his lean face with a twinkle in his blue eyes. "Ha – ye see, tew heads are better'n one even if they're only sheep's heads" – a remark incidentally my father sometimes used to make.

From the standpoint of having sufficient engines by 1964 to restore and keep in good condition, the collection could be said to be complete. Not from the variety of road using machines, however, because there had been in the 1900–1940 heyday of steam, thirty or so builders of traction engines, apart from those who specialised in rollers and waggons. But the Sentinel, distinctive as it was, was by no means the last to come to Bressingham. Collector's disease is usually an ongoing thing and curable only by bankruptcy or death, and if winter storage space under cover was now very inadequate, it was no deterrent when news came of another engine for sale at a bargain price. Such a price was relative – not to former prices, but to what was an obviously a rising demand. I used the original price when new as a basis. If one in need of repair or restoration cost about £500 as did most traetion engines when new, then almost any figure below that now would be enhanced in line with inflation, which had jumped ten to twenty times in 50 to 60 years and was still rising. When therefore an 1890 Fowler single cylinder came on offer for less than £100 it would have been foolish not to accept.

It was in rather poor condition boiler-wise having been used for many years to steam sterilise soil on a Norwich nursery until condemned for insurance purposes. The fact that we had five locally built Burrells already was likewise no deterrent to having another which had spent years at a sawbench in North Norfolk. This also had a weak firebox, but as a type or model it was a replica of the much lamented Bella, cut up for scrap during my absence. Then came the offer of another Portable. It was built in about 1910 by Youngs of Diss when Jack Clements was working there. He said that all fourteen engines they built had boilers made on the spot from the long since extinct but top quality Lowmoor iron and Bressingham, so near to Diss, was the obvious place for it as it was the only one left.

In due course a Robey/Tanden Roller somehow found its way to Bressingham. This was also distinctive enough with its inclined boiler and only one roll back and front on which to run. Not so old, built in 1924, and modern in certain respects, with skimped finish that would not have been tolerated by such as Burrells. Roger said such Rollers were built for levelling off tarmac and he'd heard of them toppling over when road conditions were uneven.

Much later, and at a much higher price, came the opportunity of adding a magnificent heavy haulage Burrell. '*The President*' had been turned out as a Showman's in 1906 but the owner had fallen down on his payments by instalment to cause Burrells to recover it and sell it again to a contractor stripped of its adornments, canopy and dynamo carrying platform. At 16 tons it was more massive than *Black Prince* with hind wheels over 6 feet in diameter and though sprung there was no indication of the wheels having been rubber tyred.

Bertha, *A Burrell Compound. This was the first engine acquired in 1961, to spark off the museum project.*

Princess *steams along the garden railway.*

CHAPTER FIVE

WHEELS AND DEALS

A relatively sudden attack of collecting mania is liable to lead to errors of judgement if pursued with undue haste. It is also liable to cause some mental conflict when time, money and expertise are all in short supply. Dwindling resources, and the raised eyebrows of some members of the family can, however, result in missing a bargain to become a cause for bitter regret later on. This was certainly the case during that hectic period acquiring a collection of engines whilst realising that they would be a major attraction to visitors to the garden. In declaring my belief that these old-timers would prove a good investment, it was with tongue in cheek, knowing I'd never wish to part with any. In any event, 10 years later, I gave them away when worth 10 times more than they cost.

Several other engines did in fact come to Bressingham during the next three years, but not to stay there. The popularity of rallies was so great that it could be seen as a means of raising money for charitable causes. More visitors and more frequent public openings were already making more gate money available for this purpose and my offer to the Norfolk Traction Engine Club was to hold a Bressingham Rally later in the summer, provided half the net receipts were paid into the special bank account from which it was my pleasure to make donations to the causes of my choice. Space was a limiting factor and, apart from a dozen or so other engines owned by Club members, 10 of mine were in steam with only three acres on which to parade or compete. It began with a parade headed by *Black Prince* and over 20 engines winding their way between the big trees on the meadow was an impressive sight. Races between engines were an event featured at some rallies but it would have been dangerous here even if I'd not been dead against the practice. But there was a slow race, as well as an obstacle course inside a ring encircled by ropes and straw bales. And a tug-of-war between scores of people trying to haul an engine back from the direction the driver set it to go was quite exciting. He

The Tidman Centre Engine, before being placed as the power unit for the Rounabout.

cleverly let the pushers think they were winning sometimes and then laughed to see them outpulled as he gave more steam. The crowd of about 5,000 was obviously well pleased and the event was repeated in 1965. Numbers attending increased and, with perfect weather, so many turned up in 1966 that a tail-back queue of cars a mile long in each direction caused such problems and disappointment for some that we decided not to make it an annual event but to extend public open days to twice-weekly instead.

One new venture as a deviation from a regular or conventional way of life is apt to open the mind beyond first expectations. Other doorways appear as enticing openings. As an added attraction, a set of steam roundabouts had been hired for the rallies and proved to be very popular. They appealed to Flora as well as to me, but if its organ fascinated her, it was the pretty little centre engine which made the wooden horses prance which took my fancy, with childhood memories welling back. To see one such engine advertised some months later in the *Eastern Daily Press* needed no excuse for me to set off at once to Burnham Market on the north Norfolk coast. The owner had not long since bought it from someone who had snapped it up as a relic from a showman who had switched to electricity on his set of gallopers. It was built by the long-extinct firm Tidmans of Norwich and had been mounted on a low chassis so as to tow it to rallies. Now, without much haggling, the necessary cheque was made out to become, I believed, more settled at Bressingham with the first thoughts that some day it might serve its proper function there.

"What about a little railway?" asked the Tidmans' erstwhile owner, pointing to something else he had for sale. There in the shadows was a miniature locomotive, sleek in its green livery, eight feet or so long but little more than a foot high. "Just what you need, isn't it?" he continued, as recent thoughts flashed again in my mind. Those thoughts had revolved around ways and means of finding money for restoration and maintenance of the traction engines. Reluctant to divert gate receipts, all earmarked for charitable causes such as the NSPCC and medical research, fare paying passengers on a little railway appeared as a feasible solution and in keeping with steam preservation. The Tidman purchase had brought my bank credit too low to consider the little locomotive as well, but once it rose far enough, then a railway would have to be a priority.

The Revd Stebbing called a few days later, asking me to take over *Bessie*'s sister ploughing engine, named *Cissie*. It had proved too big a job for him to restore with no-one to help, and the thrill of driving *Black Prince* to haul it the 15 miles for the reunion was mine as driver. In answer to my enquiry about a miniature railway locomotive at a reasonable price he replied, "It's strange you should ask me that. Only last week an old friend of mine said he wanted to find a good home for one he'd spent years building. Such things aren't much in my line but I can find out more about it if you wish." A week or two later Flora and I made ourselves known in person to Commander Robinson at his home near Bury St Edmonds. He was in a wheel-chair and was obviously a sick man. "No choice for me now but chair or bed," he explained huskily. "Our clerical friend no doubt told you it's a 7½ inch scale model of the Tilbury Tank with the name *Thundersley* – all the LTSR locos had names of places on the Southend route. It took me 12 years to build as a hobby and then I crocked up and couldn't ever finish the paintwork. I'll never do so now. My housekeeper will let you in the shed which used to be my workshop. Not been inside it myself for six years."

I spent a few evenings painting it at Bressingham. It was such a perfect model but, along with wistful thoughts that it could not possibly pull coaches with paying passengers to meet the need, I could not help thinking also of the man who built it. He had accepted his affliction and approaching death with a fortitude and philosophy which I doubted very much would be mine in such circumstances. Such thoughts were humbling but were no deterrent. A railway had to come and so locomotives larger and more powerful would have to be found. But a tailpiece describing how the Tilbury Tank became lost to me has to be included here. There was no safe place to put it on show to visitors and, after about a year in seclusion, a telephone call came from a man who had been trying to track it down. He explained in pleading tones that he was infirm and had for years been searching for a model of his favourite locomotive to cherish for the rest of his life. It meant so much to him and he gave me assurances that it would be well cared for after his death. I was touched by his earnestness and what seemed to be sincerity and decided to let him have it at a very modest price with a small profit on the figure I'd paid. A few weeks later a Christie's catalogue revealed that the new owner had entered it to be auctioned in a special collective sale which no doubt left him with a handsome reward for the con-trick he had played on me.

The need for money to offset costs was becoming quite acute, but still, rather obstinately, I stuck to the self-imposed principle of giving all gate receipts to charities. Yet, an opportunity to profit from a deal was missed, however, on another occasion about that time. The two partners in the now closed down firm of Doran Brothers, contractors at Thetford, had each retained a steam roller for old time's sake. Having come to know one of them, Mr Brown, when he found a chimney for the Foden, I made a casual enquiry about the two Burrell Rollers – the pick of their fleet. Following his explanations he offered first refusal at £100 each should they decide to sell. Three years later came the offer at the same low figure. But the old reluctance to become a dealer prompted me to say that, as I did not really need them, I suggested some budding enthusiasts should be given the chance. I learned later that they went to a man who very soon parted with them again for at least five times their cost.

But a helpful profit was made when I was asked to part with the Marshall. Even Jack had been baffled by the persistent thump on the crankshaft and had given up trying to cure it. A farmer from Somerset came one day to say that he'd been searching far and wide for this same type – a double-crank compound, because his father had owned one for years and a replacement would be of sentimental value. In spite of being told of *Beatrice*'s fault, he offered a substantial profit for what had cost me £150 only a few years before. Prices had soared but his was over the top and I let it go, little realising how much higher they would still advance in a few more years. Rarity value was certainly being enhanced by the widespread enthusiasm and nostalgia for steam. Traction engines, and even the slower, less versatile steam rollers were fast becoming objects of envy or admiration and to own one was almost a status symbol for men wishing to indulge in a somewhat outlandish hobby. Maybe this filled some obscure psychological need, but for me that need was now filled to overflowing with over a dozen road-using engines of various types, none of which could possibly bring in the revenue needed to keep them in good running order. They were never built for fare-paying passengers and a try-out with a farm harvest trailer with straw bales for seats had shown

Back to Life, the Bressingham Traction Engines on Show.

Tractions Engines in retirement, first on right is the Robey Roller.

that this form of transport behind a steam engine was not an acceptable substitute for something built for passenger carrying. When it became clear that the little Tilbury Tank would not be up to passenger carrying I began studying the *Model Engineer*. This was not only to learn a little about miniature locomotives but in the hope of seeing one more suitable to our needs being offered for sale. Two 9½ inch gauge were offered in May 1964 at an address in Bexleyheath. A round trip was quickly organised to visit Chelsea Show and some gardens in Surrey and Kent and we arrived by appointment to see Mr Hamment, the owner. He had been running a little railway in nearby Danson Park but, having fallen out with the Council, had decided to sell out and emigrate to Bermuda. *Princess* immediately appealed, though its gauge was a little below the more usual 10¼ inch. It was at least four times the size of the 7½ inch Tilbury Tank and weighed a ton with tender. Modelled roughly on the LMS Princess Class of 4-6-2 Pacifics it could, we were told, easily pull five little trucks full of children – with adults too if need be. Sensing some advantages as a buyer in these circumstances and with assurances from Dick Simmons who had driven and serviced it, my offer of £750 for both engine and trucks was accepted with a hundred extra for half a mile of track.

The other engine also appealed, for it was a 2-4-0 made to resemble an old time American Western, complete with cowcatcher. But again the extra would have put me deeper in the red at the bank than I felt prepared to go. A boost to incentive to get the *Princess* running with all speed lay in the fact that a new open season had just begun and its route had been decided upon for months, though no preparations other than mental plans had been made. This route was from near the entrance of the private drive to the house from the main road and to run parallel with the latter. The first stretch was meadow, in use as a car park on open days. Beyond, to the west, were the five acres of garden flanked and screened from the road by a shelter belt of oaks, elms and hollies. Following this closely, it would not impinge on the garden and would even be out of sight in places where hollies and conifers intervened. With a loop at each end it would make a travelling distance of nearly half a mile – just about right, and my luck was in again, especially as Dick Simmons said he'd like to move house so as to be within easy distance to drive and service the *Princess*, not that Jack and Roger were daunted by a new aspect of steam power.

They were in fact enthusiastic but, having already much to cope with on the type more familiar to them, they welcomed Dick's special skills.

My own most urgent task was to lay a track for the *Princess*. The rails were delivered with some of them fixed to metal sleepers in poor condition. It was the Jubilee type, having both rails fixed together by this means. A barrow load of odd pieces of wood had to be found rather than delay assembly by acquiring and cutting up ex-railway sleepers. Staples were used to fasten rail to wood and my eye, rather than boning rods and a spirit level, was used for the same reason – with every indication that a passenger service would be well supported, haste was essential. Having laid well over 200 yards of track which included a little curve to pass under holly trees that almost made a tunnel, a downward slope became perceptible. A spirit level confirmed it to be about 1 in 40 and reluctantly the decision to postpone the completion of the route with its embanked end loop had to be made.

A buffer stop of a large lump of wood was let into the ground where the track ended. Better begin a service on little more than half the distance than delay opening for several weeks. Besides, test runs with the little train were essential, discounting the anticipated delight of driving. Roger took the first trip with Jack squatting on the tender and me in a truck behind. They had made sure that the injectors and mechanical cylinder oilers were working, as well as the safety valve. All went well, chuffing along to stop well short of the buffered end on the slope. When Roger suggested I took over for the next trip, after reversing back to the starting point, I squeezed my backside into the little seat on the tender to find leg room also cramped. No matter, the thrill was the thing and the steaming anthracite smoke wafted back sweetly into my face.

"Don't forget there's no brakes on the loco," Roger had warned as I blew the shrill little whistle and opened the regulator. There were brakes on the tender and, having reached the beginnings of the slope, I began to screw down the handle. But instead of slowing down, the speed was quickening though I'd already cut off steam, but, there, only 10 yards ahead was the end of the line and the makeshift wooden buffer stop. The tender brake was obviously not holding against the pull of gravity as I realised I'd lost control and was well beyond the point at which Roger had stopped. Perhaps the buffer would cushion the now inevitable impact – but with a horrifying thud *Princess* pushed it aside as I strove to stay in my seat. Over the rail end she went, front wheels digging into the soft soil and coming to a stop with only the rear driving axle still on the rails.

Full of shame, memory returned of the Fowler's mishap, with a melted fusible plug and with *Princess* even more acutely head down, I opened the valves of both injectors to make sure that this did not happen again. Standing aside puzzling how to re-rail her, mixed feelings came when I saw Jack and Roger coming.

"Brake wouldn't hold," I said contritely.

"Hm! Doesn't do to rely on a brake when you're heading for trouble. Reversing lever back and steam open is the only way to stop. But you'd gone too far downhill no doubt." Jack was quite casual about it I thought and when Roger backed up his statement I had no defence, no excuse. Twenty years before *Bella*'s front wheels had slid down a ditch bank because I'd overlooked or failed to apply the emergency drill of putting her into reverse. I should have remembered. *Bella* had taken half a day with jacks and timber balks to right but, with the farm's digger tractor, *Princess* was to take much less and was found to be undamaged. Two days later there was no ceremonial opening of the Garden Railway. Deciding to make no charge to begin with, children clamoured for rides and by the next open day sixpences began to add up to offset the running costs. By the end of that summer the track was complete to allow the little train to run round each looped end in a continuous circuit and a rough sectional shed was knocked up as a loco shed with points to gain access to what had to serve as a station. The Garden Railway was, according to accepted classification, a miniature railway, well under what was or had been used other than for pleasure alone. Believing at first that, as such, it was the most appropriate as a revenue earning adjunct to the collection of road using engines, there was a case for another such attraction. Proof having come that the Garden Railway would show a profit, a suggestion was made that there would be a demand for another miniature line not far away, so when an offer came to buy a 7¼ inch gauge 4-4-2 Atlantic at a price I could reach, I could not resist it in spite of warnings that such a gauge would have a low carrying capacity. Here it must be admitted that my judgement was warped by a frustration which had come unex-

The first railway at Bressingham, 'Princess'.

pectedly as a damper on more expensive plans in mind. The little Atlantic, however, was not a satisfying compensation, as I very soon found out. As a trial, a track was laid on the grass inside the hedge which flanked the drive to the house. It was less than a hundred yards but still enough for a trial. With steam up, two pairs of hands holding on to the tender were enough to prevent it moving. The driving wheels slipped and that was it.

Words of wisdom from Roger and Jack were again largely ignored when, having quickly sold the Atlantic, another larger one was offered on loan by a collector who had no track on which to run. It was named *Peter Pan* and as a 10¼ inch gauge was reckoned to be much more powerful that the three inch difference in gauge would suggest. Given a longer run it should also give a much better performance too. For a year or two I'd seen possibilities in running a railway around a two acre lake I'd made in the late 1950s. It was well away from the garden area, on the edge of the fen and was already of scenic value – as well as for fishing and skating – now that trees, rushes and water lilies were well established. This was the place for a second miniature railway, to make an interesting route of nearly half a mile. There was only a foot or two difference between land and water level on the south side and, to add colour and interest, I dug and planted a strip for moisture loving plants. The north bank was much higher, which made a sharpish down-grading curve at one end easy but not so at the other, despite it being a less severe curve. Whether the route was clockwise or anti, these curving gradients were seen as the one threat to successful operations as the track was laid.

Peter Pan had the distinction of being the locomotive behind which King George V and Queen Mary had ridden when visiting the 1924 Wembley Exhibition but she showed disapproval of the less than easy graded track round the lake at Bressingham. With only a dozen or so passengers behind it pulled away smartly from the makeshift station and speeded along the fairly straight and level north bank, slowing down for the curve at the far end of the lake which was made long and narrow because Robert, Adrian and I enjoyed speed skating. Picking up speed again, *Peter Pan* was a pretty sight, chuffing away on the strip between the water and a high thorn hedge, but its two sets of driving wheels were no match for the up gradient to the station. They spun in a slip, out of friction contact with the rails and passengers were asked to get out and push. As a trial run it was a disappointment. An empty train ran next and, when various adjustments to curves and gradient had been made over the next week or two, the 'I told you so's' were heard from those whose knowledge and experience I'd tended to ignore at the outset.

Peter Pan was delivered back to George Milligan, its north Norfolk owner and when one of the experts on miniatures said a larger engine with three sets of drivers might succeed where two from a smaller steam capacity had failed, the search for one such was obviously the next step. A 'wanted' ad in the *Model Engineer* led to a 4-6-0 being acquired. It was modestly priced at £600 because its service at Rhyl had been closed down. With pretensions of belonging to the LMS Royal Scot Class, it was much larger than *Peter Pan* but not so long-boilered as the 9½ inch *Princess*. The difference in gauge between the two was said to be due to varying applications of scale interpretation as between American and English model engineers. On the matter of scale, however, *Princess* had been specially built with wheels of a smaller diameter to provide more traction for the heavier passenger loads than if made exactly to scale.

This factor was to prove crucial in the renewed effort to run a service round the lake. With a longer heel base than *Peter Pan*, the curves at each end were widened to the limit - restricted, as they both were, by nursery roadways in regular use. A sharp curve not only slowed down speed but was bad for wheel tyres and flanges. The first trials with *Prince Charles* were with all this in mind and a tell-tale screech on a curve had to be taken as a cry of protest, likely to be acute if pulling a load. As far as humanly possible, this additional venture into miniature railways must be made to succeed. The Garden Line was netting £20 to £40 on each fine open day and I chose not to tot up what the Lakeside Line had so far cost, without any returns, in terms of track, rolling stock and, above all, labour. Even if my own labour in levelling and track laying had been discounted, several others had been involved to a lesser degree.

Try as we might, and did, *Prince Charles* proved to be only a little more efficient than *Peter Pan* had been. From the first, I'd persisted despite the hints and opinions coming from those with more knowledge and experience. Apart from Roger and Jack, who were better able than I to overcome the inherent disabilities, such as Dick Simmons and the BR expert, Geoff Sands, had pointed to the basic trouble. The curves were still too tight and could not be opened any more. Added to this was the inevitable up gradient at the end of the circuit. This had caused the more powerful *Prince Charles* to stall when pulling a load and I hadn't the heart to charge fares to passengers, some of whom – the men of course – had to be asked to get out and push for the last 30 yards. The experts had said that the basic cause of the trouble was that both locomotives were exact scale models. As such, the diameter of their driving wheels was too great for a track with slight curves and gradients if these were out of scale in keeping with main line tracks designed for passenger and express running. For them there was a maximum gradient capacity for adhesive traction and a minimum curvature radius, below which coupled driving wheels would safely negotiate especially at speed. Because of this, the performance of *Prince Charles*, which was a six-coupled locomotive, was little better than the smaller, four-coupled Atlantic.

QED but it was not the first time in my life that the cussedly obstinate streak in my nature had caused me to come unstuck, even if sometimes obstacles had thereby been overcome. Once again I'd had to learn the hard way.

Princess, *proves the popularity of steam-hauled riders.*

CHAPTER SIX

BREAKING OUT AND BOOKING IN

Frustrations in one area tend to make one break out in another provided incentive does not falter. But no matter how inspired and determined one feels, someone else's mind can turn the scales from failure to success by coming out with an idea which had never occurred whilst one was trying to keep to a fixed ambition. When it became clear that the little Garden Railway would be a success my sights switched to the two acre lake. An encircling track would be an ideal setting, except for inevitable gradients and sharp curves. In discussing the idea with Roger, he had emphasised these snags and, in his quiet matter-of-fact way, come out with the suggestion of going for a two-foot gauge railway, if a route could be made to traverse just one side of the lake, to make a round trip.

At first this two-foot gauge idea did not appeal. Built as they were for industry, I imagined that such a railway would lack attraction to visitors and, due to lack of space in the vicinity of the paddocks used for parking, the two-foot gauge track would have to be in the adjoining nursery fields. Belatedly I began to see advantages in this. The visitors were barred from access to the rather widespread nursery for a variety of reasons but there were some very good reasons for taking them round part of it by train. Apart from the added attraction of seeing the plants and flowers we grew, it would stimulate interest even if at that time we were strictly wholesale only. And they would probably pay for the privilege of riding behind steam, however unlovely the locomotive.

These thoughts germinated into embryo plans very soon after the Garden Railway began operating. I'd been obliged to charge the cost of rolling stock and track to the business. This was not only because I was personally skint, but because our accountant had pointed out that, whereas the gate receipts were being paid into a separate bank account for charitable causes and therefore not subject to income tax, passenger fares would be taxable. This was annoying, though understandable, since up to now steam ventures had been my personal affair and quite separate from the business, of which I was still the head. But my sons Robert and Adrian had joined in and, with Flora, were now directors with a share-holding and in due course would be taking over the management from me. It was therefore only fair that I should obtain the approval of all three before embarking on another outlay especially as the boys at that time were beginning to edge themselves in with their own ideas and plans for expanding the business as I had done at their age, having been my own master at 24, at some sacrifice to my father. There was therefore every reason to be diplomatic and to choose the most opportune moment at which to come out with my new project.

The three of them, Flora, Robert and Adrian, were returning from an evening out in Norwich. Having enjoyed it, the timing was propitious but their reaction was unexpectedly and unanimously adverse. Even the suggestion that a railway would be useful as a means of transport within the nursery made no impression. Their arguments were that my somewhat outlandish and overgrown hobby should not impinge on the nursery business, either territorially or to any extent financially. They had all been more tolerant already at some cost to the boys' ambitions and to Flora's loss of privacy on open days, and there had been times when they had refrained, out of consideration for me, from being critical of my deviation on to steam engines. Presenting, as they did, such a united front, I could not argue that such a project would soon prove a good investment because, successful though the Garden Railway was so far, it would take a year or two to begin to pay back the capital outlay. I knew well enough that shortage of capital had been a constant anxiety ever since coming to Bressingham, especially as some neighbouring land had recently been acquired.

Having ruled the roost in matters of development and finance for over 30 years, it was not easy to give in but, in accepting their protests with as much grace as I could muster, it still chafed and, as well as the drive to see what outlet another miniature would provide, there was an underlying confidence as well as determination within, that this setback would only be a temporary postponement. Contact was made with a man I had heard of, who already owned one of the North Wales' slate quarry locomotives. It was installed on a very short length of track in his garden and seeing it strengthened my longings. It was not ugly and would not put people off riding behind it in spite of being purpose-built for industry. Then Roger came back from a holiday in North Wales to report that most of the Penrhyn Quarry locomotives had already gone at a mere £100 apiece, six having been exported to America in one batch. Such news was goading and in late November, nine months after being persuaded by my family to give up the idea, Roger and I set off for North Wales.

Snow began to fall near Kettering and a little skidding made me decide to leave the car at Rugby and go in by train rather than become stuck in a Welsh snowdrift. It was a decision I soon had cause to regret. On reaching Bangor we had to take a bus late in the day to Bethesda only to find that there was no snow there and no overnight accommodation to be had, so back we went to a hotel in Bangor. Next morning we were shown the remaining locomotives in a long shed, narrow and dark, by Mr Stevenson the quarry manager. Apart from telling us that none of the six was in good running order, he said that they had to go regardless – for scrap if need be – and that all the tracks had to be likewise taken up in favour of lorries for transporting what slate was still to be quarried. It was a vast complex with miles of track on different levels, but the main purpose had to be pursued, with me holding a flashlight whilst Roger made his inspection. The best of the batch, Roger reckoned, would be *George Sholto*, named after one of the old directors of the company which, we learned, had invoked the longest strike of its workers in British industrial history. To save their own time and energy those workers had long ago built their own passenger trucks and these too were standing in the yard to be scrapped if not sold. Before we left, they were sold along with *George Sholto*. Ten pouns apiece for the four trucks and £100 for the locomotive, which was an amount I could afford and, by not charging them to the business until they were serviceable, there could be no complaint from anyone at home. Besides, having agreed to open to the public on Thursday afternoons as well as on Sundays to relieve the pressure of visitors, it also offered more incentive to accept that, with so much evidence of the joint attraction of gardens and steam engines, their objections were losing validity.

Roger and I had been standing beside an engine which was already spoken for and not for sale. This would have been our choice, but, not far away, there was another, or what had been another before the boiler had been taken off. Having no further business beyond enquiring about some rail, to be told that a scrap dealer had bought the whole lot, I asked for another look at the forlorn chassis still bearing the name *Bronwllyd*. It was unlike any of the others, in having six wheels and outside cylinders and motion, with the relatively modern Walschaerts valve gear. It was these features which had appealed. All the others had been 0–4–0s, mostly built by Hunslet, as was the 1909 *George Sholto*. These had outside cylinders but inside valve gear – Stephenson's Link Motion. They were, moreover, saddle tanks, giving them a somewhat humped shape but *Bronwllyd*, built by Hudswell Clark of Leeds in 1930 had, we noticed, a well tank between the frame, thereby leaving the boiler sleek like a proper railway locomotive.

"It's for scrapping," explained Mr Stevenson. "Nobody's shown any interest in it and when the boiler was condemned it went for scrap and wasn't replaced. The bearings are pretty rough I remember – but you're not interested, are you?" Roger, knowing very well that I was, said we might be lucky enough to find a boiler somewhere which would fit the frame. When told that only the scrap price of £30 would be charged, *Bronwllyd* was added to the cheque I was about to write out.

A part of our plan was to go on to a remote part of the Anglesey coast at Camaes Bay. Roger had learned that the recently deceased Captain Hewitt had secluded a large collection of relics, amongst which we might find some items of value to us. Having no car, it seemed to take hours to reach Amlwch by bus, and then we had to take a taxi for the remaining 10 miles. By the time we reached the desolate place it was dark and blowing a gale. A caretaker guided us from shed to shed to see, with the aid of candles and matches, the fantastic collection which the eccentric recluse had amassed. There were model engines and ships, machine tools and mechanical relics as well as stuffed birds and books. But nothing was for sale and an inventory was being made for all to be sold at auction.

Back at last to the car at Rugby and then home with no adverse reaction to my report on the trip. In the mail had come an offer of another narrow gauge locomotive, as a result of previous enquiries. It was an Andrew Barclay 0–6–0 which had worked in a West Midlands steelworks until, on becoming redundant, it was sold to a newly-formed society of steam enthusiasts with a view to finding somewhere to run it for pleasure. The letter offering *The Doll* came from the principal stakeholder and was made because the little society had fallen apart leaving it, he said, as something of a liability. A final decision had, however, to be made but I was promised first refusal if disposal was confirmed at a meeting early in 1966. Having a television programme with Percy Thrower early in February, it would make a tedious journey to the BBC Birmingham studio more attractive to inspect *The Doll*, shedded only 10 miles from there, if the offer was confirmed in time.

It was, and the very reasonable price of £200 was an added incentive for the journey, knowing that an inspection would be little more than a formality. Flora came too and once again waited patiently whilst I looked over what I was already determined to buy. As industrial engines went, *The Doll* was quite pretty in her green livery, rough though this was. Following Roger's and Jack's usual methods, I prowled, tapping and poking at salient points without much suspicion of any weakness or wear. Being a little larger than *George Sholto*, I guessed her to be eight to nine tons in weight and, after half an hour, decided without really knowing that she was in reasonably good order. The gauge had been given as 2 feet but it did not occur to me that this was appreciably different to that of *George Sholto*, nor did it occur to me to measure the exact distance between the wheels, back to back. Elated as I was and knowing that *George Sholto* would not be in running condition for some months with several repairs needed, the overriding urge was to prove the statement true that *The Doll* was serviceable by steaming her at Bressingham.

There it would need track on which to stand, let alone on which to run. The scrap merchant who had contracted to take up the 15 miles of rails at Penrhyn had not shown much interest in my offer to buy some of it. Having been told that before he came into the picture we could have helped ourselves for less than £10 per ton, this was an added regret for not acting a year ago on the narrow gauge project when a better choice of locomotive was available. When told that the price of rail, delivered, would now be £22 per ton, there was no other option than to accept. It was necessary for someone to go to Penrhyn to daub what lengths and points were required to avoid trouble for both buyer and seller. This was a task only Roger could perform. The spring rush on the nursery ruled me out but the track laying would be my job once it eased. The track arrived one Saturday afternoon in two decrepit lorries and, explaining to the drivers that there was no-one but me to help them unload it, one said gruffly that no help was needed and where should they tip it? Within 10 minutes they drove the empty lorries away having tipped the track out on a patch of grass near the nursery office, close to where the station would be for what was planned to become the Nursery Railway. Eighteen tons of second-hand rail made a vast, untidy heap. Each 18 feet length – some curved and with three fixed sets of points mixed in – would be difficult to extract and sort out, weighing as it did about 28lbs to each yard of single rail. When a bill came charging it at £28 per ton, it provoked a challenge. A telephone call to the supplier brought a curt reply and no reduction but, on finding his original written quote of £22, prompt payment was made at that figure which, in law, he could do no other than accept.

The route had already been decided upon, in consultation with Robert and Adrian. It was to be a modest half mile to encircle the hub of the nursery, including the four acres of beds in which Alpine plants were grown in pots. It was also to skirt the lake by making use of the already-graded north bank. A brick culvert over the little stream which fed the lake, had been a pleasure for me to build the year before but there was an up gradient to the north at the far end and there were sharp curves to be avoided. With no knowledge of *The Doll*'s capacity for taking curves, it had to be a case of trusting to luck where restrictions prevailed. The need for haste was to some extent in conflict with that of ensuring a sound track bed. The soil itself was not difficult to compact but the only readily available ballast was gravel from local pits. This consisted mainly of water-worn flint stones, smooth to the touch and inclined to scatter when tamping down until or unless soil was mixed in with it. Being flat-bottomed rail, dog spikes were obtained to fasten it to the ex-BR sleepers sawn in half, each length being bolted together with fishplates which came with the rail. My main helper was Don Hubbard who, with Ben Francis, came back in the evenings to lay the rail on the sleepers I had laid during the day.

George Sholto had arrived, well before the rails were delivered, on a low loader which also carried the remains of *Bronllwyd*, followed by another delivery. This consisted of the four old and rather decrepit workmen's trucks and three slate trucks. The latter were the first to come into use, for, with the first pair of rails in position, they were not only useful for extending it by carrying further track-laying material but also as checks for the gauge. This proved to be nearer 1 foot 11 inches rather than 2 feet but this apparently was the standard Penrhyn gauge and a gauge rod of that length was made and used when laying the track. When Roger came back from dumping the rail required, he took what he called a 'Jim Crow' from the back of his little van, with the remark that it would be needed. It was. He had foreseen that some lengths of rail would need to be bent for curves and this curiously named tool was vital for such a purpose – especially as the new track would have four 90 degree bends in making the complete circuit. With two iron claws and a large screw to be wound down with a crowbar, bending took place, not all in one place but in several, to produce the required even curve.

Hard labour though it was, for me especially, for about 10 hours a day during those five weeks of June and July 1966, I found it enjoyable. It was rewarding too at the end of each daily stint to survey what additional length had been achieved. For Don and Ben it was a change to tackle a job very different from what they had done during the day. And, if Roger was preoccupied with repairing *George Sholto*, his support was that of a man who had longed to add narrow gauge to his lifelong involvement with steam. The arrival of *The Doll* had caused some concern. As part of his assessment of it – having had to rely on mine and my less than expert inspection before it came – he measured the exact gauge. Finding it to be a full 2 feet, he advised a compromise between the Penrhyn 1 foot 10 3/4 inches and this 2 feet for the new line. As he said, it was somewhat critical because in trying to make it wide enough for *The Doll* as motive power,

Preparing for 2ft gauge. The soil from a new ditch forming the raised bed.

Laying sleepers and rails through a wood.

there would be the risk of the passenger trucks' wheels coming off.

By mid-July the half mile track was complete. So was the station platform, the line having been graded so that the people could step into the trucks more or less at the same level. *The Doll* had been given a steam test, since *George Sholto* was not quite ready because Jack was having to make several missing parts on the lathe. All was well as she began hauling the empty trucks on a trial run. There were squeaks of protest as she took each curve with driving wheels tight within the rails, but Roger took them slowly as I kept an eye on the trucks behind, the other critical factor. One circuit made, we then made another, at a little faster pace and still no trouble. The next day the passengers arrived and, with a train waiting at the station, it was heartening to see how they began to hasten aboard at a shilling per trip. This was in spite of the jolt which passengers were subjected to as a result of slack coupling chains between each coach whenever the engine was given more steam. By mid-afternoon they were queueing for rides and here at least came vindication for me as ideas surged for making the most of what was such an obvious success. But with the last full load came trouble we thought we had escaped. A sudden check to the engine and shouts from behind, with people in a lop-sided coach gesticulating in distress. No-one had been hurt and they were taking the sudden jolt in good part, as we learned on walking back to the offending end coach which had one of its two sets of wheels resting on the gravel track bed.

Apologies went with the request for the 15 passengers to get out. Only two elderly ladies objected, fearing to be lifted down to terra firma as some younger ones had been, by men who made a joke of it. There was no lack of volunteers to lift the thing back on rail, then a lusty voice or two shouted 'All aboard!' with the offer to lift any lady unable or unwilling to take the risks attendant on clambering up to show immodest exposures.

It was no joke for Roger and me with fears of a fault which would be hard to remedy. There were no more trips for us to make that day. Next day, we walked back with our tools and, because I could not bear to admit defeat, insisted that safety might be attained by fastening down the rail more securely with extra dog spikes on the tightest curves. Some of those already used were loose or half way cut from the pressure of *The Doll*'s wider gauge and lengthy coupled wheels of an 0–6–0. With hope rather than conviction, the new service began again three days later and again visitors flocked to take the ride, with the combined attraction of steam and seeing so many plants along with glasshouses and frames en route. The coaches were rickety and had no springing beneath the toast-rack wooden seats and floors and, being crowded to, if anything, more than capacity appeared to be all part of the fun for adults and children alike.

Then, just as I was feeling glad after a dozen or so trips that I'd insisted we try again, down it went. It was almost a repeat of the previous mishap and the same means were used to put the matter right and continue the ride. Not for long, because at the next tight curve another coach became derailed which effectually put an end both to the day's running and to any hope that *The Doll* could be the regular motive power – ever again.

The latter stood out starkly as inevitable. Its width of gauge and length of coupled drivers had nudged out the outer rail on the curves little by little and this was why the derailments came later in the afternoon in each case. It offered a gradually decreasing rail surface on which the truck wheels following could travel on, until one had none at all, and no amount of dog spikes on the wooden sleepers could stand up to the pressure of *The Doll*'s relentless, heavy flanged wheels trying to straighten out the curves we'd made.

With only a brief cancellation of the new service, *George Sholto* emerged to take over, having to be hauled from the still makeshift workshop with a tractor, over the gravelled yard to the rail track, with painting unfinished. It was just in time for the 1966 rally weekend. Staying with us was a fully-qualified locomotive engineer I had come to know and like. This was Geoff Sands, who at the time had just been appointed Locomotive Shed Master at Salisbury, having previously been at Crewe. He took a great delight in driving *Sholto* round the little track, at the controls of a locomotive so different to others he had formerly driven on BR routes at ten times the speed. But the crowd on these two exciting days was so great that, at 50 passengers or more each trip, it left as many who wished to ride but failed to do so. As an augury for the future prosperity of the line it was good. But the rake of four ancient coaches were beginning to disintegrate. Nails

The 1909 Hanslet, George Sholto *on the 2ft guage*

and screws and patches on old, half-rotten timbers were failing to hold them intact Another expense loomed and local help was enlisted to make a new set of five to hold at least a hundred passengers Redundant skip bogies from quarries were located and bought and these became the subject of joint consultation with Charley Knights and George Garrard.

Charley had just been called in as a skilled carpenter to fit our house with thief-proof devices. On a stormy night following the last of the two rally days, a break-in occurred which none of the 10 sleeping occupants heard, but though they took my strong box and a few more items, the record two days' takings had been too well hidden for them. But it was a nasty experience and from then on fullest possible security became of paramount importance George Garrard had also made a good impression with his welding skill on a number of occasions and now he had to adapt the skip bogies with swivel axles to make five eight-wheeled chassis, almost twice the length of the old Penrhyn workers' stock. Not that they would be in use until another season came It was up to me to ensure that they were then ready because the possibility of running two trains on an extended nursery line had burgeoned into a compelling urge to make both a reality in time for the 1967 openings, and positive moves had already been taken to make sure of this.

The offer of another Penrhyn Hunslet locomotive had come quite unexpectedly. Someone unknown had bought the 1883 *Gwynned* only to find he lacked the means to restore and use it. He had apparently handed over the matter of selling it to someone else and it was his letter to me that set off enquiries as to price and condition and where it could be inspected. Answers were evasive and, although highly suspicious when told that an offer of £150 had already been made by someone else, a chance had to be taken with this to back up my plans for expansion. At only £160 the risk was that it would cost several times that figure if the boiler and firebox were unsafe. But when it arrived, to find that only retubing and some welding in the tubeplate were needed as well as attention to the motion, the prospect of a second train on the Nursery Line was good enough to repeat the order for coaches *Gwynned* was also a saddle tank type, a little smaller and less powerful maybe than *George Sholto*, but neither Roger nor Jack had any doubts about it being able to pull a load so long as gradients were not too steep. There was only one up gradient on the projected longer route but it was more severe than on any part of the existing track.

Amongst the facts I'd already learned concerning railways was that tight curves over rising ground were above all to be avoided for easy running. It was one thing to feel the power when giving extra steam for a hard pull, with the resultant sharp blasts coming from the exhaust with plenty of smoke, but it increased wear and tear on the locomotive enormously as well as costing more in fuel. The new extension meant abandoning the lakeside track and, regrettable though this was, the line had to take a much wider reach into the fen fields of the valley bottom, curving towards the east it would run straight beside a ditch for the length of two eight-acre fields and then turn north, it was when it left the fen level that a quite steep rise began – about 1 in 20 for a hundred yards. The only way to overcome this was to stretch and so reduce the rise, by making an embankment on the level to ease the slope. That autumn Ben, Francis and I began the task as loads of subsoil were dumped at the foot of the rise, surprising how much it took to make a stable base for sleepers only 4 feet long on which rails could safely be laid.

The supply of more rails for the extended track had presented problems Enquiries led to two possible sources of supply, one of which was only 20 miles away at Claydon Cement Works near Ipswich, but no decision could be given for several weeks until the company made up its mind whether or not they were to be transferred to another works now that conveyor belts had made them redundant. The other source was much more definite, the dock area, at Port Penrhyn, serving the quarries was also to be redeveloped and here was track in abundance to be cleared by the purchaser. This was likely to be a scrap merchant if I did not act quickly, it was late autumn but, with Flora and our two little girls, we headed for Wales with the hopes of a little holiday in their minds and of a deal for rails in mine. The system was, however, almost buried so that only the upper surfaces could be seen but, suspecting that some might not fit in for size and weight for what we had already, I could but guess which to mark for others to lift. A few days later a car full of helpers, including two newcomers and Roger, were on the job, they worked hard for two days and then Roger telephoned to report trouble. Some of the lengths I'd marked had proved to be unsuitable as well as being heavier and so more costly since the deal had been on a weighbridge tonnage basis. There was no alternative but for Roger to use his own discretion and in due course another 30 tons of rail arrived in a variety of lengths and sizes. Within days of it being unloaded came word that the cement works' track of well over a mile was available, sleepers and all for a much lower price.

With ideas that further extensions to the Nursery Line and possibly a second route was quite a possibility for the future, the offer was too good to let slip. On a visit of inspection the cement works' manager even offered to save us the trouble of dismantling and lifting – but he did not specify the means of so doing and, guessing it would be by his quarrymen, I refrained from asking. But when the first load arrived much of it was twisted and it was obvious that fishplates had been cut with acetylene and the track itself lifted by an inconsiderate bulldozer driver. But here was track enough for another two miles or more and an old diesel loco used in the quarry, now also redundant, was purchased, with expectations of needing such a machine for track laying and maintenance.

So much activity, both mental and physical, devoted to steam in general and narrow gauge in particular was forcing my mind into departments I was having to learn to switch suddenly from one to another – as the need arose. Matters so diverse as field drainage and fishplates, plant propagation and engine painting, seed sowing and steam pressure crowded in, to leave too little time to relax and take a look at what I was neglecting in matters closer to home. The period called for drive and energy and no thought or evidence of being over-stretched or negligent came to mind. Enthusiastic as I was with the narrow gauge extension, a request to give a home and a place to run *Maid Marion* had to be accepted as a matter of course. My key helpers were also in favour for they too seemed to be infected with a similar enthusiasm.

Maid Marion – a little Hunslet from the Dinorwic Quarries had been bought by a small band for preservation. They came mainly from Lancashire and, having lovingly restored it, found they had nowhere to enjoy running it. They had in fact made a tour of the three or four preserved lines of this gauge but none offered scope or encouragement to the running of a little group whose knowledge and experience of steam fell far short of their enthusiasm. This became evident when the maroon-liveried 0–4–0 was put in steam as an extra on Whit Monday 1967. What with leaking glands, faulty injectors, inexpert firing to raise pressure to the required level, it made a belated entry into service and even then found it difficult to keep the second train going on the now extended line in turn with *George Sholto*. This extension, however, was not an unqualified success as a well graded line. True, the over-tight curves had largely been abandoned or eased, but the up gradient, after leaving the fen level, was still pretty steep in spite of the embankment Ben and I had made to ease it. Being straight, I'd reckoned on being able to open out to gain enough momentum to reach the upper level, but this ploy had its snags. An engine creates a sharper draught in the firebox as the regulator is opened wider. Here, in order to take the rise, it was sharp enough now and then to pick up live sparks liable to fly over the driver's head and on to the passengers in the open trucks behind – which they did not consider as part of the fun in riding behind a steam engine.

George Sholto, *coming out of the Engine Shed.*

'Gwynedd' *built in 1888 preparing for a days work.* Background: 'George Shilto'.

CHAPTER SEVEN

LOVE'S LABOUR LOST

In spite of mishaps, miscalculations and the misgivings on the part of others concerned, there was evidence enough that a narrow gauge nursery railway would be a success. Not, however, to serve the needs of the nursery business. This had been more of an excuse than a compelling reason to go ahead with it, pointing out that tractors churned up access headlands and roadways when lifting plants for orders. In using such means of persuasion, there was no ambivalence, nor was it necessary to point out possible snags – such as a railway being unlikely to cover more than a fraction of the whole area, or the reluctance of staff to hand-carry trays of plants more than a few yards to it. But the salient fact for me was the need to cater for the steadily mounting number of visitors. It was the only valid reason, and the costs of extending the role of steam in a horticultural setting would thereby be justified. A spur line was, however, laid to enter the packing shed but, apart from testing its potential with the Ruston-Hornsby diesel, it was, in the event, never used again. The diesel was useful for trackwork but it had no self-starter and had to be pushed to get it to run under its own power. Having only *George Sholto* as fit for service in 1967, we sometimes had to use the diesel for passenger haulage to make me long for *Gwynedd* to come in. Somehow diesel was an ignominious makeshift. But *Gwynedd* was taking up most of Jack's and Roger's time with months of tedious work. Its copper firebox was very thin and day after day Roger laboured on it to patch it, whilst Jack painstakingly fabricated its many badly worn and missing parts. The saddle tank was far too gone to patch and its curving shape very difficult to replace with new metal. A very costly job, was George Garrod's verdict. He was a journeyman welder and I took his advice to make a straight- sided tank to run on a quarry bogey as tender for water and coal, leaving the faulty saddle in place so as not to spoil *Gwynedd*'s good looks. And almost twice daily, as I walked to the office, where, beside the Nursery Line station, was what was left of *Bronwllyd*, still boilerless and forlorn, came the sad doubt as to whether or not she would ever come back to life.

To have *Gwynedd* in service was becoming more obviously top priority and *George Sholto* was having to leave passengers behind to be first on for the next trip. With boiler work completed, tests had to be made. At that time no official inspectors were required and so long as we could obtain insurance cover without a boiler certificate, there was no point in going to the extra expense. Beside, Jack Clements, Roger and George were not skimpers. They knew what to do to make boilers and fireboxes safe and all three had learned by practical experience, since narrow gauge locomotive boilers were much the same as those for traction engines. Jack especially was sceptical of official boiler inspectors' abilities and quoted instances he remembered of them faulting an engine on a minor technical matter of construction but failing to find a more glaring and dangerous weakness. Appointed as they were by insurance companies, almost invariably their experience had been gained on marine or industrial boilers and some Jack had known were not in his opinion competent to pass judgement on other types. The method of testing a repaired boiler such as *Gwynedd*'s was simple. Closing all possible outlets such as washout plugs and steam pipes, the boiler was filled to the brim with water and with a special hand force pump more was forced in to make the pressure rise in the gauge glass. It was known in advance what would be the correct pressure under steam before the safety valve came into action. With safety valve held down, the pump could double pressure if need be but, when it reached 50–60% over designated pressure and held there for a few hours, it was reckoned to be safe enough to be used in steam.

If repairs or retubing had been made, it was often necessary to keep up the water test pressure by additional strokes of the pump at intervals to counteract minor leaks – what engineers call 'weeps'. These would appear where valves, glands, tubes, etc. were not quite tight enough, to be noted down or chalk-marked for further attention. Tubes were seldom all perfectly tight first time. After being driven in through holes in the back and front tube plates, special expanders were inserted to make them swell into their tube plate holes until no possibility of leaking existed.

Where 2 ft and 15 inch tracks cross, the 1883 Hunslet 2ft 'Gwynned' *has right of way.*

Next came the steam test which, incidentally, would be less effective for tracing leaks because of the heat making the metal expand. But there were places where steam could escape through an imperfect gland or fitting not previously revealed by the water test.

Gwynedd's boiler passed both these tests. The next stage was to lift it back on to its chassis, but first came another task calling for great expertise, that of setting the valves in tune with the pistons before the final run. It was Bill Harvey, BR loco shed master at Norwich, who volunteered to do this tricky job and, having done it by patiently adjusting the rods which opened and closed the ports in the cylinders till perfection was reached, he then offered to make a brass cover like a large helmet over the steam chest atop the boiler. This was mainly for appearance's sake for it had been missing when *Gwynedd* arrived and there was every reason why she should not be deprived since *George Sholto* had one already. It took Bill several weeks to make, hammering out the sheet brass to fit over the dome which had to be first encased in insulating material to avoid loss of heat at the point where the steam collected to be sent down to the cylinders when the regulator handle was opened. Not that either Jack or Roger could not have set the valves correctly, but they respected Bill Harvey as they did Geoff Sands as experts in railway motive power, and we were all keen to run a new railway successfully.

By this time – 1967 – ideas of not only extending the Nursery Line were close to being uppermost in my mind, but to having a second route as well. The scope was there. The public attraction was fully in evidence, and we had rail enough in stock. All we lacked was sufficient motive power, even when *Gwynedd* came into service. The introduction of two trains very soon revealed the necessity of making another platform. The existing one was only long enough for one, and it would be an obvious advantage to build another close behind to become the arrival platform at which passengers would alight. Without blocking roadways there was just enough room and there was no difficulty in making the platform raised above line level in keeping with the existing platform. Then, whilst one train filled up ready for departure as the other was en route, its arrival at the rear platform would be the time for the one in front to leave. It worked and, at busy times, enabled double the number of passenger to ride. Here was another good excuse and perhaps reason for a second route. *Maid Marion* was only steamed about once a month and only by her shareholders. It had become redundant with our own two locos and now had no service to perform unless another track was made.

In earlier times at Bressingham the wilder parts of the fen and its wooded areas towards the south drew me to take walks on summer evenings or winter Saturday afternoons. In times past I'd take a gun, but now it was a spade or an axe. The spade for easing the flow of ditch water to improve drainage; the axe to sever ivy where strangling the trees. More lately, when Anthea and Jenny were old enough to walk down the Causeway to the woods, it was a pleasure to find their interest in nature and to make a little stick fire. But it was none of these pursuits which prompted me to prospect a route for a new railway line. The Causeway had been made long before because the valley was often flooded in winter – mainly because the infant River Waveney, forming the Norfolk-Suffolk boundary was not in the lowest part but squirmed through rising sand soil. On this grew pines, oaks, box and rhododendrons. The new line must find a way through this thicket, so dense in places that nothing but greenery could be seen, but it was the best part of a mile from the farmyard, now fast becoming a yard for engines instead of stacks.

The Causeway was quite narrow with a deep water-filled ditch on the west side and another, now half-filled with waste nursery soil and sand, on the east. All other access to the woods was low and peaty and a much larger watercourse, which now took excess water from many thousands of acres upstream, would have to be bridged, independently of the Causeway bridge. A new railway would need a loop to bring it back to the yard again. Doubts on feasibility were expressed, though not by me, when realisation came that this was the only possible route for what would have to be named the Woodland Railway. That autumn, with other duties becoming less important, I began making a track bed from near where *Bella* used to saw wood behind the farmyard. Trailer loads of more waste soil were brought and tipped in heaps on the rubbish previously dumped in the shallow ditch on the east side of the Causeway for me to level out. Further down, the digger tractor scooped out bucket loads of soft sand from a bank near the wide stream, now called the Bressingham Drain. By Christmas, this straight stretch of nearly half a mile was ready to take sleepers but, deciding to leave bridge building until spring when water levels should be lower, I marked out the course beyond – over quite boggy ground, until it reached the point where it would enter the wood. With helpers away on Christmas and New Year holidays for nearly two weeks, the interesting part of my task began with axe, saw and machete reminding me somewhat of the clearing forest on piece work I'd done in 1949 on Vancouver Island. It surprised me not only how fiercely rhododendron bushes burned but how far they had spread out from their main rootstock. A way had to be cut through them to wind a little so as to avoid the oaks, pines and the larger box bushes. As usual, when working intently alone, hymns and psalms from choirboy days made maddeningly repetitive mental music, but the daily burn-up registered progress and it was a change to work on firm sandy soil which would need no ballasting. It was also comforting to know that the greenery – so colourful at flowering time –

which had to be destroyed in the 10 feet wide trail being made, would make new growth quickly. And that this would be the easiest of any track bed I'd so far had to grade with barrow and shovel, as was necessary, once through to a clearing at the other end of the 250 yard wood where only a few Corsican pine trees grew as the land sloped down to fen level again.

Here the whole method had to change. Some embanking was needed, shown up on a long straight-edge and a spirit level. The slope had to be more gradual and the track bed raised a foot or two above the field level. Having found soft sand to lie beneath the top peaty soil years before when pulling out scrub trees with *Bella*, the only recourse was to make a new ditch parallel to the track and so mix soil and sand together from the excavation for the railway. This involved the digger tractor and as it piled the spoil from the ditch I levelled it out with a shovel since the space was too narrow for a machine to work. I was anxious as always to take up the least amount of land, poor though it was for any crop but grass, due to bad drainage. Planks were needed to support the barrowloads of spoil but the mixture compacted well. Another two weeks of enjoyable labour brought the track bed back to form the end loop and at this point a pit was dug to provide enough elevation for the set of points needed to make the link. Then came the bridge – a lucky purchase of a Bailey Bridge section just long enough to span the Bressingham Drain, about 16 feet across, let into concrete abutments made by letting in 50 gallon tanks filled with concrete.

With my having to revert to spring work on plants, it left Ben and Arthur to lay the rails on the sleepers I'd laid. Arthur, like Ben, was getting on in years but had some experience as a traction engine driver and now had hopes of a route on which he could drive a train. The pair fell out with one another sometimes and Arthur, being touchy, was prone to walk off the job. If he threw his tools down and stalked off, having taken offence, he would mostly change his mind before going very far and return, in silence, to the task with renewed zest. By this time Don, who had been a leading plate layer on the Nursery Line, had graduated to become a painter – for both coaches and engines – becoming quite expert in his thoroughness. He had been with me since 1947 and, apart from helping me with irrigation and drainage, was in charge of strapping and nailing down boxed orders of plants and driving the lorry.

The narrow gauge running equipment had to come under the ownership of the main business for accountancy and tax purposes. Only the non-revenue earning traction engines were still my personal property. But, although Robert and Adrian were taking on more of the farm and nursery management, I was free to go ahead with narrow gauge extensions because they were making a small contribution to earnings – or would do so when fully operational.

It was, however, very obvious that steam motive power was the draw. The visiting public was no more interested in diesel than was I and, before the new Woodland Line was completed, the need for more narrow gauge engines became increasingly vital. Enquiries revealed that no more were to be picked up cheaply in Britain where scarcely any were to be found for sale at all, regardless of price. On learning that some were becoming redundant in northern Spain, it soon led to another family holiday with steam as the main object for me. That May we took the car by sea to Bilbao and drove west from there into the mining region around Oviedo, with Ribadasella on the coast as a base. Some 60 centimetre gauge locos were to be made redundant but mostly they were still in use. Some were German built, others Belgian, but their owners were non-committal and even a trifle suspicious, not appreciating any reason I gave for wishing to purchase. At last a verbal agreement was made for two which had been discarded but, although guarantees of payment were given, all follow-up efforts to implement the deal came to nothing and no replies were received to letters I wrote.

Hopes of better luck next time led to a second trip a year later, ranging much further afield including Portugal but it was much the same story. The only locos to be found, which the owner was in a mood to sell, were of a different gauge which could not be altered. To add some bitterness, I learned that someone else soon afterwards secured some well-preserved engines from Sabero. My informant wished to act as agent since he knew the manager well and agreeing to his request not to deal direct led to his losing the purchase to someone else.

But for a boiler having been found for *Bronwllyd*, the future of the Woodland Line would have been bleak. Some ex-Coal Board man-riders had been obtained, but only *Maid Marion* was available if *George Sholto* and *Gwynedd* were to stay on the Nursery Line. With the Lancashire lads coming to run *Maid Marion* monthly, Jack and Roger went all out to get *Bronwllyd* going. The boiler had come from the dismantled *Stanhope* and, although of a different make, it happened to fit the frames without much difficulty. With reduced pressure because of metal wastage, it went into service in the rich red paint I'd used by way of a change from *Sholto*'s green and *Gwynedd*'s blue, and *Gwynedd* was transferred to the Woodland Railway with Arthur Prentice as regular driver. There was, however, a problem. There had been ample space for a loop at the far end but not so at the near end terminus. A system of points enabling the engine to switch itself free of its coaches was devised. It was a triangular affair, it not only took time as passengers watched and waited, on two occasions the engines became derailed, which took up much more time to put right as well as attracting more people to watch. It was not good for our public image and, as soon as opportunity came, a loop was made around the Spinney which had previously been ruled out as too tight. The screech of wheels against rails when the train came slowly back to its station was indication enough of that tightness. Someone suggested applying oil to the worst spots but, although this eased the screeching, it encouraged *Gwynedd* to pick up her wheels and slip so alarmingly that dry sand had to be applied to counteract the oil.

Gwynedd has been my preference for driving on the Nursery Line. Though less powerful and by name less masculine than *George Sholto*, she was more to my liking, mainly because her water feed injectors were more reliable than *Sholto*'s original type. *Gwynedd*'s injectors, fixed to the faceplate, had been missing and new Penberthy's had been fitted. Apart from that, she was both responsive and reliable but when *Bronwllyd* came in at last – four years after I had taken a pity on her as well as a liking at Penrhyn, no doubts existed as to who her driver would be. It was her build, with all the motion exposed and with boiler mounted well above the frames that gave her a certain elegance. The footplate too, was higher off the ground than the Hunslet's, but she was so well sprung that no juddering was felt travelling over the somewhat uneven rails. She was, however, inclined to bounce. This was due to the three axles being close together, leaving considerable weight overhanging back and front where there was a massive cast-iron buffer beam. With the brake on for a down gradient, the bouncing was apt to be disconcerting, especially as the brake winding lever was behind one when driving. If having to face forward when the brake was needed, one had to be careful, for it was all too easy if using the left hand to turn the handle in the wrong direction, until one realised the brake was not coming on.

The lack of success in Spain was worrying. Even if we now had a loco for each of the two Nursery Line trains, and one regular one for the Woodland, it made sense to have spares in case of mishaps or needful repairs. More or less constant enquiries eventually brought an offer from a man near Hamburg. He was a rail fan with an eye to business and had located and bought a 60 centimetre Orenstein and Koppel which he invited me to go and inspect. With artist David Weston for company we were met by the owner to see what was, by British standards, a not very attractive locomotive in a contractor's yard. Unlike those we had already, it had a somewhat ungainly cab and a chimney bulged at the top as a spark catcher. It gave the impression of brutish power and, though there were doubts about its weight of nine tons being on only two axles upsetting our track, I decided to part with the £400 asked, having no other options in view.

As a reserve, it was used only a few times and, when later an offer to swop it for a smaller O & K came, there were no regrets in letting it go off to Wales, where it was to work a new narrow gauge operation. *Eigau*, too, had a cab and, to the extent of being liveried in BR green, was partially Anglicised. It had in fact been a Penrhyn locomotive, having been restored to good running condition. In service it proved to be rather temperamental but we now had four in running order, but I was still uneasy, believing that there should be one reserve for each route. When another offer came from Germany we decided to take it on the strength of the owner's guarantee that it was fully serviceable. And so it proved to be when *George Sholto* had to be withdrawn for a new boiler to be made. The newcomer was an 0–4–0 Schwarzkopff, and was as Germanic as its maker's name. This too had a cab, but almost all the drivers, including the volunteers, preferred cabless engines. They were cooler in hot weather and less draughty when cold and windy, and even with the risk of a soaking when wet one felt less hemmed in and better able to see around and therefore have better control.

Eigau *a German built "Orenstein & Koppel" 2ft gauge.*

The Schwarzkopff, which was naturally named *Brunhilde* was bought to offset another abortive trip abroad. On learning that there might be a few 60 centimetre gauge engines in Austria, I took boat and train to Vienna and finally traced one lying at a merchant's who bought and sold machine tools of all kinds. A quite small, low to the ground 0–6–0 with no maker's nameplate, had an instant appeal for its compactness, distinction and seemingly good condition. Then language difficulties hampered negotiations but, having agreed the price, no deposit could be paid because of a prevailing credit squeeze and exchange control. I promised to fix matters once home again, but asking for a *pro-forma* invoice brought no response. Becoming impatient, not even the Austrian agent I decided to employ was able to make any progress. This, and a Le Corpet in Spain were the two locomotives above all to cause some pining regrets for being unable to acquire them.

By the time hopes faded of the little Austrian ever coming to Bressingham, depressing thoughts were coming in because the Woodland Railway was not the draw for passengers we expected it to be. True, the station was somewhat obscured, but large notices as well as cheap fares were still not filling the low built, roofed and well-sprung manrider coaches. The home built Nursery Line coaches were bumpy for lack of springs, but still these were preferred by the twice-weekly visitors. The ride had been extended for the third time to bring the journey to well over two miles and fares had been raised in keeping, whilst the Woodland, at a mile and a half, was not well supported at half that of the Nursery Line fare. It was worrying and I began to suspect that it was a mistake to have a second line of the same gauge as the first. There were also lingering regrets that the scenic lakeside route had to be abandoned – not that we could have extended the Nursery Line without forsaking the north bank of the lake. As niggling thoughts continued, so crept in an inkling that a 15 inch gauge railway would have been a better proposition than either the second 60 centimetre or the 10 1/4 inch which failed to make the Lakeside circuit. But as a roughly half-way gauge between the two, there could be problems in finding a suitable route, especially if attempting to use the Lakeside as part. In any case, rolling stock of this gauge was not in the industrial category and, for the three other 15 inch railways operating in England, all had specially built locomotives. And on being informed by someone, who knew how costs were going, that a new 15 inch would cost at least £20,000, it almost cleared my mind of any such ideas.

Saturdays were not days when casual visitors could be made welcome. They were rest days for the staff, many of whom would be at work on the Sunday and, for me, Saturdays were days when on my own I could work in the garden undisturbed. When on a September Saturday afternoon a youngish man, undeterred by closed gates, was encountered, I was rather brusque in reprimanding him. He apologised but when giving his name I connected him with the Narrow Gauge Railway Society and accepted his plea that he believed it was an open day. For a little while we talked steam and narrow gauge and I showed him what we had. Having done so, he asked casually if a 15 inch would be of any interest. He'd learned that three locos along with coaches had suddenly become for sale in Germany. They had been overhauled and bought for an amusement park near Cologne and, for some obscure reason, were prevented from being installed as a pleasure railway.

Over the weekend new possibilities again opened out to become so absorbing that by the Monday a series of frantic telephone calls were being made. Yes, finally came the reply, the equipment was still for sale but others were interested, including another Englishman. Three days later I was ushered into a rather dim, ramshackle shed near Cologne, crammed with 29 coaches and three sturdy and quite handsome locomotives, despite their fading Prussian blue livery. Their history was that these 4–6–2 Pacifics were built by Krupps of Essen in 1937 to run a service in an exhibition park in Dusseldorf. After the war they were overhauled and made ready for use to serve a similar purpose elsewhere but, with steam going out of favour, had been in store for six years. The coaches were unroofed but, although a few appeared to be in need of repair, they were obviously made with no expense spared and the wood, now lacking varnish, appeared to be teak so far as I could judge. Left alone, my brain was in a whirl as I stayed on trying to assess clearly the best approach to the owner. He had already said he wished to keep one of the three for sentimental reasons. This was some relief because the whole lot would have been too many for us to use and too costly.

Only hints were mentioned of the price given in Deutschmarks, but it was enough to cause much concern. Later, when meeting the owner, the price of about £5,000 each for two sets was stated to be the rock bottom price, but still I hesitated and asked for a few hours' grace to think it over. That few hours was spent walking the streets of Cologne until midnight and after that more wakeful hours in my hotel bedroom

By morning the issue was clear. The offer would cause more regrets if I turned it down than it was likely to if it led to the two complete trains finding a new home at Bressingham. The agreement was signed with a lawyer in attendance and shipment was arranged. Finally, three Dutch juggernauts arrived one morning in mid-December. Two were full of coaches and these were drawn out and lifted down close beside the Nursery Line. The third lorry held the two locomotives – *Rosenkavalier* and *Mannertreu*. A ramp of sleepers, topped by rails, was hurriedly built as the light began to fade and the rain began to fall. The long lorry took time to get in exactly the right relationship with the ramp, for the engines were about seven tons in weight and the lorry floor was nearly five feet above the muddy road level. The main concern, once the front bogies were on the ramp rails, was that the weight as the driving wheels followed might cause an uncontrolled rush downwards since no checks, brakes or winch could be used. Robert came up with the bright idea of using our portable compressor on the locos' air brakes and, under the gleam of torches and lanterns, we watched and waited. The air brakes worked well until, with all the engine's weight on the ramp, it suddenly lurched down out of control and almost disappeared into the darkness. Then came a sickening thud as it pitched over onto its side on a curve we'd had to make to steer it clear of the lake. Restricted space for unloading had been a problem, but sighs of relief came when *Rosenkavalier* fell over to the right instead of to the left and down the steep bank into five feet of water. Checking the ramp, the cause of the mishap was found – a dip in the codged-up track had prevented the brakes from working. Once this was put right *Mannertreu* made a sedate, safe exit and by then it was nearly midnight and still raining.

All my fretting vanished once the indisputable fact of ownership was there to see next morning. *Rosenkavalier* was soon righted and the mud cleaned off. There were not only approving remarks from helpers but the knowledge that the whole lot for just over £10,000 – including £1,750 for transport – was indeed a bargain. In high spirits and renewed zest, the new route was a pleasure to survey and plan. The departure platform would be on the strip between the south side of the lake and a high tree-studded thorn hedge, and passengers would have water on one side all the way to the lake's end. Continuing eastward, it would have to cross over the Nursery Line in a coppice of oaks and birch and then curve south, bridging the Bressingham Drain, till it reached the old Waveney River, and then turn west to link up with the loop of the Woodland Railway. This link up would put an end to the latter by reducing the gauge from 60 centimetres to 15 inches. Not all the labour of laying it would be wasted, and the labour of making over a mile of new track bed would not be easy going. Apart from another bridge, an untidy, overgrown hedge would have to be hacked back and a new ditch dug to make an embankment beside a boggy fen meadow.

The two 15 inch Krupps Pacifics 4–6–2, from Cologne raising steam aided by blowers.

CHAPTER EIGHT

SEARCHES AND SUCCESS

. . . *Two Krupp Loco's, ready for work.*

An obsession, regardless of the subject, is liable to lead one to face unsuspected problems as well as fantasies. The latter came as part of the process of going the whole hog when pursuing an objective which was far from being clearly defined because it was clouded by the limitations of ways and means. By 1967 steam, as part of the Bressingham scene, had developed far beyond first one-off expectations – from one traction engine to 14 and on to

'Rosenkavelier' *crossing the new bridge over the infant river Waveney.*

operational 9½ inch and 2 feet tracks. It had been a case of unfolding possibilities as scope and public appeal brought opportunity and incentive, despite the lack of personal gain except that of satisfying a deep-seated urge. None of the engines had so far been acquired with thoughts of selling again at a profit. The convertible Burrell roller was sold to an enthusiast railwayman because it was an oddity, with front roller being replaced with the forecarriage of a threshing machine. The Marshall had mechanical faults which defied even Jack's skill to correct, and a good offer for it was accepted to help pay for a more useful engine. The 2 feet gauge *Doll* went to Leighton Buzzard for much the same reason, for it was simply incompatible with its track. All three came in pursuance of my now obsessive involvement with steam and left because, by the end of the 1967 open season, a new and very exciting vista began to appear. It came first as a glimpse and then all of a sudden, the view of standard gauge, as the most spectacular development hitherto unattainable for such an unlikely setting as a Norfolk farmyard three miles from the nearest railway at Diss.

The concept of a comprehensive live steam museum did not dawn on me until the late 1960s. Until 1967 the character and appearance of the farmstead itself had scarcely changed since I had come to Bressingham. In summer there were the restored traction engines on a hard-standing which had replaced nursery plots whilst an extra roof over a small cattle yard had become a makeshift workshop. Other additional farm buildings were for a herd of pedigree pigs which Robert had gone in for, with 80 breeding sows and, at that time, open day visitors were allowed to see where the noise and the smell came from. During these early years wistful thoughts on larger railway locomotives had to be pushed aside whenever they occurred, if only because I saw no worthy place for them at Bressingham till late in 1967 when quite suddenly the wider concept of a comprehensive live steam museum opened out.

The somewhat glamorous appeal of standard gauge had in fact been stimulated only weeks after *Bertha* came in 1961. Apart from a furtive ride on a 1500 Class 4–6–0 which made me late for school, I had never been on a locomotive footplate. Even then, it was only of 50 yards up and back on to the Cambridge-London Express as a result of some garden produce gift to a friendly driver, Mr Arblett. Forty years later it was a direct request to Mr Goodings, the Norwich area manager, which fulfilled a lifelong ambition I had hesitated to pursue for fear of rejection despite the extensive use the nursery made of BR services. I'd seen, admired and ridden behind the new Britannias and now was given a permit to ride footplate from Diss to Liverpool Street. It was a ride on which no greater thrill could be imagined, despite the noise and, at first, the rather frightening uneven rolling of the 140 ton locomotive as it charged over sets of points at over 60 miles an hour. Inspector Sands, according to the rules, was appointed to see I gave no trouble or got into trouble, and it was through him that I came to know his son Geoffrey who was, years later, to play an important role at Bressingham. But not before, whilst Geoff was loco shed master at Crewe North, was I allowed another footplate ride from there to Shrewsbury and back.

It was about that time – 1964 – that, as a committee member of the Norfolk Traction Engine Club, a discussion took place on its somewhat embarrassing surplus funds standing at the bank. Having recently learned that the last of the old Great Eastern Claud Hamilton 4–4–0s was for sale at £1,500, I suggested some of the surplus could be well used by buying it for preservation, hoping of course that the committee would agree that Bressingham would be a suitable place for it to stand as a static exhibit. The committee showed no interest whatever in the idea. Traction engines were their only interest and I was certainly in no position to buy it myself. But it niggled, especially as the offer expired in the Claud being cut up for scrap. Some months later, with a few more hundreds to my credit at the bank, I combined a lecturing trip with visits to Doncaster and Nottingham where more locos were standing after being withdrawn from service under Beeching's over-hasty conversion from steam to diesel. I walked around a dozen or more of varying sizes and classes, standing cold and grimy, yet pathetically majestic as they awaited the executioner's torch. November fog added to the depressing sight and, with spirits in decline, I realised that the cost of transport alone – Bressingham being three miles from Diss Station – would swallow most of my bank credit. Along with this came a mind's eye picture of one of those engines standing immobile at home, with no hope of putting it in steam and motion. As a dead, lifeless relic which I'd pass every day, it would be almost unbearable for me, if not for the visitors.

It was quite evident that steam alive was what appealed most to the visiting public, and then out of the blue came the opportunity to have a railway locomotive capable of being on show in steam and motion. The offer came from Northamptonshire where open cast ironstone mines were closing down. Three were available at only £200 each, together with some flat-bottomed rail. I chose a saddle tank 0–4–0 Peckett of some 25 tons weight and, being of metre gauge, it appeared then as a means of a compromise between the fanciful and the realistic. The nursery and farm entrance roadway was a straight 150 yards from the main road with a scrubby hedge on both sides. That on the west had been planted years before with young beech trees, but the hedge had inhibited good growth. Grubbing out the hedge would leave width enough to take a metre gauge track and, well before the 1968 season began, it was laid and *Banshee*, as I named the Peckett, had been repainted and tried out in steam with a view to giving footplate rides for a small fee. In between my normal work and track laying and painting, a chance conversation with someone on a train was leading, little by little, to a new and exciting development. It came not only as a scheme of challenging urgency but as an embryo vision of the kind of place Bressingham could become given luck and continuing help from those who had the power and the means to give it their blessing, if I played my part with unswerving determination.

At that time, Alan Pegler was running special steam excursions behind *Flying Scotsman*, under agreement with BR, which he possessed only when steam had almost vanished from main lines. Flora and I decided to indulge in a journey from Norwich to York behind this most famous of all British locomotives, not counting the record-breaking *Mallard*. On it I met for the first time David Ward, an executive for BR at Norwich, and a steam enthusiast. In the course of conversation I spoke of past disappointments in not being able to include a main line locomotive at Bressingham. This brought the question, had I read the newly revised Transport Act? A "no" from me led to some startling information. It was that BR's Consultative Panel for the preservation of historical relics was now empowered to allocate relics on loan to approved private museums. The existing museum at Clapham could not possibly house all those under a preservation order and in store here and there.

"I think", David smiled, "you'd stand a fair chance of getting one if you can provide a suitable building which will pass inspection – and get on the right side of John Scholes at Clapham. You might even be allowed to choose one – but there isn't a Claud Hamilton if that would have been your choice. All cut up, more's the pity."

To begin with I was invited to a little informal meeting at the Clapham Museum to meet John Scholes along with two members of the Consultative Panel, Captain Peter Manisty and Mr R C Riley. On being shown a list of locomotives to be preserved which were in store, my eyes blinked and, when asked which of them appealed to me, I could scarcely take this as being offered a choice.

The names that stood out for me on that list were *Britannia* and *Thundersley*. When I came out with them, Mr Riley spoke up to say that *Britannia* was in a deplorable condition, having been badly pillaged before being shedded at Brighton for greater safety. But Mr Scholes said, "Would you really give a home to *Thundersley*?" – from which I could only deduce that this 4–4–2 tank was languishing. My thoughts went back to the little model built by Commander Robinson, which I so heartily wished I had never parted with. And now there I was, it seemed, being offered the original 70 ton *Thundersley* on which the little model was based.

"I'd give it a good home," I said feelingly. It was then that I learned that the final decision rested with the BR Board, and must wait until the Consultative Panel had met and made its recommendations to the Board. We chatted, without my realising at the time that I was to some extent being vetted in the process, and for good reason since I learned also that mine was the first application of a private nature. These three gentlemen were fully in the know about every aspect of locomotive and rolling stock preservation and, as I knew so little but wanted to know more, I listened very intently to them. The discussion went back to *Britannia*. As the first of the BR Class 7s to emerge it was the one designated for preservation under the guiding rules. It was a pity, they agreed, that such a rule applied in this case, because No 70000 was so rough, when others of the class were in much better shape, especially 70013 which had been overhauled at Crewe only a few months before – the last steam locomotive to go through the shops. A cloud of uncertainty came over this conversation. Rumours were afoot that steam was to come to an end before 1968 was out and, though it was known that No 70013 was to be used on special steam-hauled trips until then, rather than on regular service, it would, in the prescribed course of events, be sold for scrap after that unless someone could purchase it outright for preservation. A Mr Cheetham was mentioned, whose role under BR it seemed to me, was rather like that of Thomas Cromwell under Henry VIII. It would, I gathered, be very difficult to persuade Mr Cheetham that No 70013 *Oliver Cromwell* should be saved by the preservation order, and *Britannia* should carry the death sentence instead. And there the matter had to rest because it was time to go to the Annual General Meeting of the Transport Trust, which all four of us were to attend.

A few weeks later, with a couple of hours in London to spare, I took a chance on finding Mr Scholes available at Clapham. Under his curatorship the Transport Museum there had become a fascinating place, but he had a vast amount of other work besides, with every conceivable item connected with railway history his responsibility. I was shown into a large building where huge stacks of documents, plans and equipment were stored and, among a variety of station boards, one taken from a station near Leeds was fixed above an inner door. That name was 'Scholes' and through this door Mr John Scholes came out to greet me, inviting me in for a chat. At first I began to wonder if my application for *Thundersley* had made any progress at all. But before long I learned that a strong recommendation in my favour had just been received from the Divisional Manager's office in Norwich, and it was quite evident that this was the kind of backing Mr Scholes needed to go ahead. I could see how vital it was for him to be quite sure of my ability to accept and discharge such a responsibility. I had nothing specific to ask him, but described in greater detail what my plans were for a live steam museum, mentioning that the new building was to give coverage to three standard-gauge tracks in the centre, with narrow gauge on one side and road engines on the other.

"Then you'll have room for more than one BR locomotive?" he suggested. I nodded hopefully and asked by way of a lead if he still thought it worth a try to get the preservation order switched from 70000 to 70013. He was quick to take my point. "Aha," he laughed, "so you'd like to see *Oliver Cromwell* come back to East Anglia?" "And the first Oliver Cromwell was an East Anglian too," I put in, adding that, apart from the Britannia class being my favourite locomotive, it would be rather appropriate since many had served to give a real fillip to East Anglian services. Mr Scholes agreed heartily and, after explaining again the difficulty personified in Mr Cheetham, finally made up his mind to have a try. "I reckon there's a good case," he said with conviction. "Leave it to me and I'll have a go tomorrow."

What Captain Manisty told me over the telephone three weeks later was by way of a tip in advance of official information. Not only was *Thundersley* to be allocated to Bressingham, and moved into Norfolk in readiness without delay, but the Board had also recommended that when *Oliver Cromwell* was withdrawn from service, this too should come. When that day would arrive no-one seemed to know, but for the present, the fact that it was coming must be a secret. I could scarcely believe my luck, but it was officially verified almost immediately by the Norwich Divisional Manager, and it touched me pretty deeply to realise how much sheer goodwill had been at work in my favour while I'd been chafing with impatience during the past weeks.

The closer one gets to holding in one's grasp something long hoped for, schemed for and worked for, the harder it is I've found, to remain patient. When there is nothing to do but just wait for final fulfilment, not knowing how long the waiting will be, then it's very trying indeed. *Thundersley* had been promised, and that was fine, because at the outset I'd never allowed my hopes to go beyond one BR locomotive. In my imagination, that one alone would be enough to satisfy my 'live steam museum' ambition. Now, with hopes alive and kicking that *Oliver Cromwell* as a representative of the class which, for me, was the zenith in British locomotive design, was also headed this way, I was so disturbed that I could think of little else.

A journey to Yorkshire in company with Norwich BR officials helped to keep me down to earth and to the present. There at

Hellifield, on a bleak hillside, we were shown into a large locomotive shed. Its leafy roof dripped melting snow onto the few locomotives there in store, and one of them was *Thundersley*, a long way from its original London, Tilbury & Southend tracks for which it had been built in 1909. It stood there, handsome still, but forlorn and neglected, so obviously in need of a good home. As we took a closer look, inside and out, I learned how it had been restored and painted in its original green livery for the LTSR centenary in 1956, but had scarcely been used since. Like many others scheduled for preservation it had been plundered when stored at Stratford and had come to Hellifield for greater security. Even then it was in danger, and we saw how some vandal had tried to force apart the fine LTSR crest from the side tanks with a tommy-bar. This had failed but the marks were indelibly there.

Because the Hellifield shed was not fully secure (thieves had climbed drown from a smoke vent in the roof), *Thundersley* was under orders to go to Preston Park at Brighton to join other locos in store, but now that transfer was cancelled and the next step was to get her to Norfolk. At this point a suggestion came up from members of the Norfolk Railway Society. The new shed at Bressingham would not be ready for several weeks, but the need to move it away from Hellifield to some safer spot was urgent. A lineside goods shed at Attleborough could be made available and, with a signalman on duty nearby, it would be safe. Once there, a team from the Norfolk Railway Society would undertake to remedy at weekends the ravages of time and neglect, as far as they were able. One of their members was Mr D W Harvey, a steam engineer of high repute, and he would be willing to replace the motion and attend to such fittings as the steam brake and reversing gear which, among others, were seized up with rust.

This was a splendid offer which I gladly accepted, though none of us realised how long it would take. Until the transfer of *Thundersley* took place in March I had little idea of how complicated a matter it was to tow a locomotive over a distance, but was thankful it was not I who had to make the necessary arrangements and see that they were carried out. It was only 12 miles by road to Attleborough, a small town on the Ely-Norwich line, and a little party of us went from Bressingham to see

Thundersley arrive on a March day so windy that I was glad of the excuse to leave my work in the garden. In any case, I would not have missed the sight, pathetic though it was to see a noble old steamer hauled in behind a diesel, But, unlike some I'd seen being towed to a Norwich scrap yard to be destroyed, this was to come to life again and stay that way.

The windy weather had come too late to be of help in drying up either the sodden nursery and farmland or the site of the new steam shed. It had been a wet but mild winter until March and on all sides work was behind schedule. It had taken a long time to erect the steelwork and lay the concrete footings of the shed. Holes and trenches were dug through the sticky clay mixture only to become half-filled with water overnight. Beneath the filled- in overlay the soil was sandy and I had considerable misgivings about consolidation for the weights it would have to carry. But we had to press on regardless, as far as the weather would allow. It was a common occurrence for one of our helpers working on the site to leave a gum boot behind in the sticky mud, and there were times when I was so frustrated at lack of progress that I made little runnels with a spade in an attempt to run the surface water off.

At last the time came when, with steel stanchions erected, the roof trusses, also of steel, could be lifted on. This called for a crane and, although we had left the erecting for a time in the hope of drying out, in the end we had to bring in 50 cubic yards of crushed airfield concrete to make a solid roadway on which a crane could operate. Crane hire costs are high, but a slight error on the part of the man who welded the trusses caused several extra hours to be charged. With trusses in position, our own helpers, under the intrepid all-rounder Graham who was normally an expert packer of plants, scrambled up to fix in the purlins. It was 28 feet to the apex and at that juncture March winds began to blow, making the task quite hazardous. A load of asbestos and perspex-type sheets for the roof arrived just before the first gale, and someone omitted to weight them down. In the morning most of the roof light sheets were scattered and broken, and a new portable nursery shelter was carried two fields away and smashed to smithereens.

It was all very trying. More gales blew up when the time came to place the roofing sheets. One was so fierce that work had to stop, despite the sheltered position of the building. The sky took on a peculiar colour from the dust blowing off the Fens and the sandy lands to the west, the direction from which spring gales can cause havoc, as well I knew from bitter experience of 25 years ago when, as a farmer in these bleak Fens, I'd known dykes to become filled not only with dust but also with newly sown seed and fertilizer. I had become a little more philosophical since then but my propensity for biting off more than I could comfortably chew was, it seemed, undiminished over the years.

There was no time now for musing, and no sense either in pausing to wonder why so often some fairly big projecct I'd undertaken turned out to be much more formidable when at grips with it, than when I had first conceived it. Once again the job was calling for far more effort than expected; once again my optimism was shown to be at fault.

The news that *Oliver Cromwell* was allocated to Bressingham had been decidedly cheering. It put a fresh heart into the few who could be told, but the very fact of the injunctions to keep it a close secret was in itself more than a little disturbing. Few reasons for this secrecy were given, and there seemed to be an implication that with No 70013 some doubt still existed. If its destination became widely known, then someone with influence could throw a spanner in the works with the argument that such a locomotive, famous already and likely to be more so as the last operational steamer to be run by BR, should be retired to a national museum and not to an obscure village in the heart of East Anglia. I gathered that there was to be a special last steam run during the summer to mark the closing date of the railways' steam era. The date was not yet fixed, nor was anyone I knew aware of the route this swan-song run would take. But I was warned by our official sponsors, who had worked so effectively in the high places of BR, to keep it quiet. I was not going to let them down, risking perhaps at the same time an almost unbearable disappointment.

I could at least confide in my family. Flora was still hoping for improvements within the house. Adrian had been hoping 1968 would bring the much needed new packing shed and, though Robert would have liked a new piggery to be built, he was for the time occupied with his own new house on which work was about to begin. All three had been pretty tolerant of my overriding decision to build the new shed. In a way, it had been an act of faith as far as the big BR locos were concerned, and now that *Oliver Cromwell* was earmarked, up went my sights once more.

My first hazy vision of a live steam museum at Bressingham was on the way to becoming a reality. Somewhat timidly I'd imagined that just one or two standard gauge locomotives would satisfy both my longings and the visiting public on whom its success financially would depend. But with the influential well-wishers, John Scholes and Peter Manisty, wider vistas were taking shape. They were amply supported by such practical men as David Ward and Bill Harvey and it was they who reminded me that now was the vital moment to acquire the spares and equipment, which were certain to be needed, as they were to be sold for scrap in the very near future. It was these two who said that a trip to the big steam locomotive depot at Kingmoor near Carlisle was an urgent necessity.

We travelled together by train, overnight from Euston station, on a main line which had gone over to electric traction. We were met by a little posse of officials who conducted us through vast sheds having rail tracks over inspection pits. All was empty, where not long since ranks of locomotives would have been there under repair or inspection. Before reaching the stores we were making for, were glimpses of grimy, forlorn steamers in line one behind another, awaiting disposal for scrap merchants to cut up. There were Britannias which had done service for less than 20 years along with Duchesses, Cities and Black Fives as well as freight engines. The stores revealed quantities of spares – from brake blocks to boiler tubes. But not many of the latter, which most of all we needed. Vast numbers had been sold to make fencing posts at a tiny fraction of their cost. There was heavy equipment too, and a wheel lathe and wheel drop were spoken for, which I saw as a daunting task both to dismantle and to instal at Bressingham.

It was a sad and depressing sight, and regrets were expressed by those who showed us what was left in the stores. It was difficult to know what might be needed at some future date with 70013 at Bressingham. But a selection was made mainly by Mr Harvey, the steam engineer in charge of *Thundersley*, who was one of the little party. It was the last chance, for soon all was to go for scrap at so much per ton, and I could not possibly miss this opportunity for securing spares.

Such trips were stimulating in a peculiar way. Here was I, a nurseryman-cum-farmer, with virtually no other background than the land, being shown round what had been the holies of holies of the railways as if I were an expert. When questioned or asked for comments, it was necessary to pretend to know more about locomotives than I did, in order to play the part that was now expected of me. The vision of a sizeable, comprehensive museum had opened up only a few months before but only now were its full implications beginning to open out too, the gradual realisation of a deeper involvement and commitment beyond my imagination at the time. It was becoming much more personal too and, if that meant a commitment for the rest of my life, it was to be accepted gladly, never to regret having done so. The sooner it began the better.

It was tantalising in the extreme to be given strong hints that *Oliver Cromwell* would come to Bressingham but, until this was confirmed, patience was hard to come by, especially with the warning of secrecy. *Thundersley* had been confirmed and there was no harm in publicising the fact. It was shedded only a few miles away at Attleborough. There, members of the Norfolk Railway Society, under Bill Harvey, were making it more presentable, with repairs also when it came to placing the piston and connecting rods back in position. These had been removed when taken out of service in order to facilitate towing – as it had been from shed to shed since then. A bearing had heated for lack of oil but had never been properly repaired. Because Bill was determined to put it right, the final move to Bressingham was delayed for several weeks, whereas I had let it be known that it would arrive in May. It was then that my impatience blew up until I realised no good would come of it.

Then, to make things more complicated, but adding still more to the exciting prospects – depending on the mood – came news that *William Francis* was for sale. Apart from pictures, I had never seen a Garratt locomotive, and indeed only one standard-gauge representative of this unique type of Beyer Peacock build remained in Britain. This was the one and it was owned by the Coal Board at Baddesley Colliery near Atherstone. As Garratts went, it was not a large one, weighing 60 tons or so as compared with the 200-tonners in use in Africa. Even a modest 0–4–0 × 0–4–0 would be a wonderful addition here, I thought, if only it could be acquired.

It was for sale by tender and I learned also that, when it was retired from service two years before, it was expected to go to Canada for preservation. An agreement had been reached and the nameplate had actually been sent in advance, and then for some reason the deal fell through. On learning that it was fitted with a copper firebox, my fear was that the most I could offer would be far below its true value for scrap. Captain Manisty was also aware of this and, as Chairman of the ARPS, he appealed to the Coal Board for its preservation, at the same time tipping me off that Bressingham might be favourably considered if his appeal met with success. It was all very tricky, for there was no knowing which way the ball would roll. What I did know was that the scrap value would be in the region of £1,400 and that such a figure put it completely out of my reach.

Having mentioned the matter to Jim Price, a friend with an interest in steam, and a partner in a thriving local electronic components firm, he came up with an offer of £500, having already hinted that an investment in steam would appeal to him. This was the lowest figure I guessed the Coal Board would accept if they decided, for the sake of preservation, to forego its full value. It would be a matter of chance whether or not anyone else, keen to preserve such a unique locomotive, would go any higher. As an afterthought I suggested another £25 might tip the balance in our favour just in case someone else plumped for a round £500 offer.

It was pointless, in my opinion to go and inspect. Time was precious just then anyway. We could but take it as it was if the Coal Board decided to let it go for less than half its value. With a tender form duly completed and sent in, all we had to do once more was to wait and hope – a state of mind to which I was becoming inured with anything but easy acceptance. Peter Manisty was the one to hear from, since negotiations for preservation would go through the ARPS and after five or six weeks' waiting his cheery voice came on the telephone with good news. It had been, he said, very much in the balance but, because we had good shed coverage, it would come to East Anglia rather than stay in the Midlands, where some thought it should remain. There was also a hint that, of the offers for preservation, ours was the highest – by £25. Jim Price was every bit as excited as I was. We came to an agreement on joint ownership, since transport and some restoration costs would fall to us as custodians, for it would remain permanently at Bressingham. At the time the good news came, he was laid up and it was Jack, Roger and I who hared off to Baddesley Colliery to size up the task of removal and subsequent restoration. No time must be lost; not only did the Coal Board want it out of the way, but I felt strongly the need to have a big loco on show, regardless of condition, since so many visitors were asking why *Thundersley* had not arrived. The floor of the shed, now drying at last, was levelled off with ballast. On it a length of bull-head rail was laid, while Roger and a mate went off again to Baddesley.

It took them three days to prepare *William Francis* for loading. The problem was not one of loading as it stood, for this would have been easy, had I been able to afford the charge for a transporter long enough to take its 48 feet wheel base. That would have spoiled the look of £1,000, but by separating the loco into three parts it would cost a fraction of this, even though it would involve three loads. It was not very difficult to disconnect the front and rear bogies. They weighed about 20 tons each, consisting each of a four-wheeled chassis topped with bunker tanks. Having disconnected the flexible steam joints and all else that held the articulated vehicle together as a unit, there remained the boiler and cab as the centre-piece with no wheels. A frantic hunt round for standard gauge bogie trolleys was finally successful, and these Roger had taken to Baddesley. It was the task of jacking up the centre to clear both ends which took the time. The boiler then had to be lowered onto the borrowed bogies and secured for the journey. Such movements have to be carefully planned in advance, with thought given to the correct sequence to ensure that the object is the correct way round when unloaded. The rear portion – tank and coal bunker – arrived first and was pushed to the back of the shed. The boiler and cab, weighing a good 25 tons, came on a longer low loader and wet weather was causing some worry over the approach to the shed.

Low loaders resent sharp corners, and one that could not be avoided was over a culvert. Seeing the risk of the rear wheels overhanging, if not dropping into a wide ditch, we shored up with a dozen or more sleepers. The driver surveyed the route on arrival and said he didn't like the look of it but was willing to have a go since there was nothing more we could do to improve it. As the low loader's rear wheels cut across the corner, sleepers began to slip under the weight, towards the ditch. Foreseeing disaster as it heeled over, we shouted to the driver to stop but, instead, he revved up and drove on. How that boiler stayed on, straining at its chains, tilting over so alarmingly, I'll never know. But it did. "And if I'd stopped", grinned the burly driver afterwards, "you'd have had the job of raising your engine from the bottom of that ditch. Keep going is my motto when that kind of danger comes – but I must admit it was touch and go. I could see what it looked like in my driving mirror and knew what would happen if I didn't make a run for it."

10 Ton Burrell Roller, of 1920 built in nearby Thetford.

CHAPTER NINE

FROM LITTLE TO LARGE AND A SECRET NIGHT JOURNEY

The summer of 1968 was one of the wettest on record for East-Anglia. Rain played havoc with our preparations to be ready for the big locomotives and there was still no certainty that *Oliver Cromwell* would be included. The yard was cluttered with stacks of rails, including sets of points, and great heaps of ballast for much of July. The slope down to the new shed was impassable for normal farm traffic because this demanded rail tops to be at ground level and not raised above as was normal practice. There were visitors to consider who could not be expected to step over exposed rails and sleepers. The necessary excavations had caused problems all along. When work began in June our own digger tractor was expected to break through the hard ground surface of the yard and when its toothed bucket failed to do so we had to steam the largest Burrell roller, fitted with its Hosack scarifier to crack up the flinty surface first. Having made a good beginning with a trench 30 feet wide and two feet deep, there came a thunderstorm which left it nearly full of muddy water which held up the work for a few days.

The first excavation had in fact been close to the new locomotive shed where, some years before, there had been quite a wide ditch, which I suspected had been a moat serving an ancient dwelling long since demolished. This old ditch had been a nuisance and before filling it in a quantity of unburnable rubbish, including glass, cans and old barbed wire, had been dumped. Because all tracks from the shed had to cross it, out the rubbish had to come, to be dumped elsewhere and to be replaced down to hard bottom with lumps of concrete once a drain had been laid.

This was one reason for a worrisome delay. Another was that conflicting advice had been given regarding the levels inside the

The only standard guage Garratt left in Britain, shown here after restoration.

shed. I'd used my own discretion so far in making it dead level but, having no experience of heavy locomotives, decided to seek expert advice. One BR track expert suggested that it would be best to ease the 1 in 45 slope of the yard outside, and there should be a lesser one inside of about 1 in 100. "All very well", Jack Clements observed, "but what happens if a brake fails on a 100 ton engine backing into the shed, eh?" The outcome of such a thing needed little imagination. If buffers heavy enough were placed at the back of the shed, a runaway engine could damage itself and, if a buffer failed to stop it, then it would certainly burst through the concrete block wall – beyond which was a drop of four feet on to soft ground.

Jack had made this doleful comment after work had begun on making the recommended slope, taking ballast from the back to raise it gradually a foot higher at the front in keeping with the expert's advice. Then came John Scholes for his long awaited inspection, along with Peter Manisty. This was just before *William Francis* arrived and their comments on the spaciousness and security were good to hear. But when an explanation was given on the problem of gradients, both men thought it a mistake. "It's not enough slope", John said, "to check a runaway engine and you'll have trouble sooner or later unless it's dead level. It would never be safe for a man to be underneath an engine for servicing unless wheels are chocked securely and it could be very dangerous." This made sense and so back the floor ballast had to go to the original dead level I'd first decided upon when I was not even aware of all the factors at the time.

Despite their positions of influence, neither John Scholes nor Peter Manisty was able to relieve my nagging anxiety over *Oliver Cromwell*. They were all in favour of it coming to Bressingham as a fitting place for its retirement from main line service and were intent on doing all that was in their power to see that it did. Both were also emphatic that what they had planned should remain a close secret lest some other party with power and influence with the British Railways Board should persuade the latter that 70013 should go elsewhere after its last run. This run would be by way of a swan-song journey – the last steam- hauled train under BR management. It was believed a date early in August would be chosen – which meant several weeks more of uncertainty to be endured, during which period the yard with its multiple tracks and turnouts must be well and truly laid regardless.

Then, in July, it became public knowledge that this eventful last steam run would be from Liverpool to Carlisle via Manchester, hauled by *Oliver Cromwell* double-headed with a Black Five on 11 August 1968. With fears persisting of a last minute change of plan as to the final destination of No 70013 I decided it would be, to say the least, unwise to take a couple of days off to travel on it for fear of an anti-climax and chagrin replacing the thrill. It was, after all, a blessing in disguise that *Thundersley* had not been ready to move from Attleborough. In spite of my impatience then, now it would be a considerable saving in road transport costs for both locomotives to come at the same time. First tentative enquiries about transport had been made months before, knowing that no ordinary vehicle could carry such loads. It came as quite a shock over the telephone to learn that it would cost at least £1,000 to carry one large locomotive the three miles from Diss station.

Three or four other heavy haulage firms I approached had nothing large enough, but a fourth responded eagerly. This was that of Sunter Brothers of Northallerton, and a letter from Peter Sunter to say they would gladly take on the job especially because of his own interest in steam, was cheering indeed. Eventually I was able to tell him which other locomotive besides *Thundersley* was due to come, knowing that the secret would be safe with him. When he came in late July to survey the route we were still struggling against the rainy weather to have the tracks laid and tested. By the first week in August the complicated system of rails and turnouts – three tracks from the shed merging into one – was almost complete. Help from outside had been not only welcome but essential for such novices as we were in laying standard gauge, bullhead rail needing chairs and keys and a crane for lifting points into the correct position. This rail weighed 95lb per single lineal yard, against the 28lb of the simpler flat-bottomed variety we'd used for narrow gauge. Those of us on the spot all helped as labourers, ramming ballast under the sleepers with shovels, lifting them first with crowbars and finding out what it was like to be railway navvies and platelayers in a hurry.

On Sunday 11 August, whilst *Oliver Cromwell* was on its way north to Carlisle with its special train, we steamed the squat little Beckton Gasworks engine No 25, not for show but with a but with a purpose. Up and down it went and though only 22 tons in weight, the axle load as an 0–4–0 was enough to settle the tracks firmly over, not only each of the three tracks leading into the shed, but on the extension we had also made as a single line curving through the little tree studded meadow. To obtain a worthwhile length it had to curve sharply, and to reduce the gradient a cutting 3 to 4 feet deep had to be made for much of the 120 yards' extra length. By that Sunday I'd been told by our constant friend David Ward the carefully laid plans and timings of *Oliver Cromwell*'s movements following its arrival at Carlisle. The veil of secrecy had been tightly drawn for John Scholes had insisted that nothing must hinder its exit from Kingmoor loco shed, knowing that the question on the lips of almost every passenger and others as 70013 was taken off, would be its ultimate destination since it was not going back on the train it had brought.

On its way south again with nothing but a guard's van behind, those in charge of each section on the route were to know only that something special was to pass that way at a specified time. It was to be guarded all the way with Mr Cogger – John Scholes' chief assistant on the footplate with a relief man in the guard's van. When it finally arrived at Norwich after its 350 mile journey it would be in the charge of our BR friends there who had done so much towards bringing *Oliver Cromwell* to the place where it had begun its service when new in 1951. The recent stresses and pressures, along with mounting excitement brought me a buzzing headache and sleep that Sunday night had to be induced by a Mogadon. Flora had remarked on how difficult it was for her to get through to me. "Not that I've been able to for weeks, come to think of it," she added. "And other people have said you seem miles away nowadays." Muttered excuses from me, somewhat aware that I'd not been easy to live with of late, and then came the question of whether I was going to see *Oliver* come through Harling Road station on its way to Norwich. It was only 10 miles away on the Ely-Norwich line and, although I knew the expected timing there.

I was not at all sure what effect the sight of it would have upon me and could not therefore make up my mind. Still fearful of some untoward hitch despite the elaborate plans, I telephoned Norwich for news on the Monday morning. And good news it was. Except for being half an hour late, all was well and 70013

Oliver Cromwell *arrives at Bressingham.*

Thundersley *newly arrived.*

was due to pass through Thetford station just before noon. "No need for secrecy now", I told Flora, "and we'll go to Harling with a welcoming party, of family and helpers would be appropriate." On the way Flora chided me for fast driving – for the first time she ever remembered doing so – with the reminder that we had plenty of time. Just as we reached the station the signal went down. "We might have missed it if I hadn't hurried," I muttered. But it was only a diesel-drawn freight train and for the next 20 minutes time passed slowly. Then the bell tinkled and the down line signal came on again. When the dot in the distance became recognisable, with smoke to prove reality and no mistake, the trouble I'd feared – and the reason for my hesitation about coming – began to afflict me. Swallowing hard, trying to hold it down as the magnificent locomotive came nearer, slowing down and seeing at last what I'd imagined and hoped for so eagerly, was too much. It seemed to take my breath away as it came fully into view, its moving rods almost idling at about 15 miles an hour. "Come on now," I told myself, "no place to let your feelings erupt with a score of other people on the platform. They won't understand if you can't keep your emotions under." The fireman gave a wave and a smile and, when the driver gave a long musical whistle as he opened the throttle again, it was the end of my emotional struggle. Walking head down towards the far end of the platform, up came the sobs and I let them come freely for several minutes. The others back there might think it odd and might ask Flora what was amiss but Flora would know and maybe Robert and Adrian would guess. When at last I rejoined them no questions were asked and no explanations needed to be given. My tensions had vanished and, if excitement remained, they were no longer fraught with anxiety.

We saw *Oliver Cromwell* again tucked away outside Norwich Thorpe station next day, hidden between two loco sheds. It had already created quite a stir on arrival the day before with television coverage, pictures and reports in the *Eastern Daily Press*. That was all good publicity now and the only remaining anxiety was the mere fact that it was still 25 miles from Bressingham and getting it the last three miles could be very tricky. Only 25 miles and two or three days separated the dream from the reality. Surely there could be no slip now between cup and lip.

Until the final move came, 70013 would be under the loving

care of Bill Harvey, the Loco Shed Master whose skill had brought an improvement to all 58 Britannias, built as the standard BR express locomotive after nationalisation. In 1952 he had schemed an alteration to the valve motion which gave smoother, more economical running, first to those under his charge at Norwich and then to the rest of the class. "I'm delighted," he said feelingly as we stood together on the footplate. "I've looked it over and I reckon it's in good shape. But it's sad to think she's the last ever to be overhauled as she was at Crewe and now it's all diesel. And it means a lot to me to think that this old friend has come back home and will stay in Norfolk. Being a steam man for over 40 years, I'd also like to think that if you need any help and advice, then it's yours for the asking. These engines will undoubtedly bring a lot more people to Bressingham, but they'll be a big responsibility and more so in years ahead as boilers and fireboxes need attention, as they will."

Three days later another visit to Norwich was called for. To set off at 11.30 pm was not only an unusual time, but the means of travel was also unusual and never likely to be repeated. It was midnight when I left the car in the deserted yard of Attleborough station, to be greeted by five men already there – comprising two members of the Norfolk Railway Society who had smartened *Thundersley*, and three BR officials all of whom were to make the same journey. We went across to where *Thundersley* stood, looking infinitely more cared for than when first seen at Hellifield last March. The only contribution I had made was to lag the steam chest above the boiler with asbestos cement so the domed cover could be replaced. And now she was ready and waiting to take her long-deferred journey to Bressingham.

For an hour we waited and chatted whilst Bill Harvey, meticulous as ever, made sure that every grease or oil box and bearing was topped up. The night was quite chilly with a waning half moon shining dimly through wispy clouds. The mail train charged through and then came the distant throb of another diesel to prove that the main line was clear, for this was the reason for our waiting. It stopped and shunted one of its two brake vans on to the up line and then backed down the siding and coupled up to *Thundersley*. With one more shunt the short train of one diesel, two brake vans and one 60 year old steamer set off at the regulation speed of 15 mph for Norwich.

For me it was an eerie journey. There was no need to talk in hushed tones but we did – those of us in the front brake van. After all the waiting, all the worries and hectic work over the past months, the occasion could have been one of conviviality but this was not the mood prevailing, which was more like those of conspirators on a darkly secret mission. From outside, above the low throb of the diesel came the staccato hissing of *Thundersley*'s wide open cylinder cocks, since the pistons of a cold engine act like air pumps and that air had to be allowed to escape. This was one reason for the restricted speed and when we stopped at Wymondham a thorough check was made of moving parts against the risk of some bearing becoming overheated. All was well and on we went, slowly enough to see in the wan moonlight the misty cornfields flattened by the storms of recent weeks, which gave farmers no chance to begin harvest. What had promised to be a bumper year had gone into reverse and what was usually the drier side of Britain had this year become the wettest.

Standing outside in the open end of the brake van it was quite cold and I went inside to join Mr Cogger. As Mr Scholes' assistant he had returned from Clapham to carry out his duty to safeguard the two locomotives all the way. Chatting quietly, he voiced his fears that before long the Clapham Museum would have to move, he knew not where, which was unsettling for all concerned. Then rounding a bend in a cutting we saw the twinkling lights of Norwich. The railway yards outside Thorpe station were still brightly lit and here and there a man on night duty stared hard as we passed. Coming to a halt, the bulky outline of *Oliver Cromwell* loomed across the tracks to give me a tingling thrill at the sight. We all climbed down to make a little group discussing the final stage of the journey, orders being given and taken. For those of us not under precise orders, the mood was changing to one of subdued excitement, though for me it was a strange feeling of unreality – as if this was a scene I was witnessing without in fact being there in person.

As a terminus station of in and out, whichever route was to be taken, a double check was made as to the correctness of order in which the two locomotives were to be placed. At Diss station they had to be tender first for haulage on to Sunter's road transporter so as to offload at Bressingham with their chimney ends facing north away from the new shed. At last all was ready and, with the addition of *Oliver Cromwell*'s 70 feet length, the double-ended diesel chugged noisily as it took on the extra 140 tons load. Mr Cogger beckoned me, as I hoped he would, to join him on the footplate of 70013, even though he might well have exceeded his authority in doing so. It was by way of proving that there was to be a close relationship with my favourite type of locomotive and not just a pipe dream. Gaining the rise on to the main line south the rhythmic hissing of open cylinder cocks was now doubled. A last look at the still sleeping city, with the first break of day from over Mousehold Heath showed the slender spire of the cathedral stabbing the sky. Rounding the bend in the cutting, bridged by the highway, I wondered if the lights of the car just crossing it would pick out our strange cavalcade as we came out on to an embankment. As the driver, I would have jammed on the brakes to watch, but here I was in a far more favoured place on the footplate. A little herd of young cattle further on shied away as we passed, to run off with their tails in the air. Pigeons flapped noisily from coppices which echoed the sharp hissing from the cylinders. It came out under such pressure that leaning out it could be seen almost as if it were steam, in spurts ahead of the fascinating Walschaerts gear motion.

Although we were running late, no greater speed than 15 mph was permitted and a stop was made at Tivetshall to check the bearings for the last time. Bill Harvey was still with us as responsible for the mechanical aspects and said that, all being well, we would be clear of the main line in time for the first morning train at Diss, now only 10 miles away. The line was now dead straight and it was light enough to see the outline of the grain silos beside Diss station long before we glided in. Little groups of people were already awaiting our arrival and cameras were clicking before we came to a stop. When stepping down from the footplate it was as if all the anxieties of the past few months had never been and, despite missing a night's sleep, I felt on top of the world – apart from being hungry. So was Mr Cogger and, after watching the needful shunting manoeuvres into the siding prepared for us, we both went back to Bressingham for a hearty breakfast. On our return the roster previously arranged for the locos never to be left unguarded was already in operation. The prevalence of thefts by souvenir hunters was well known and volunteer guards of Round Tablers by day and the recently retired PC Edwards by night would deter such would-be robbers. Perhaps it was an unnecessary precaution, for, as it happened, there was a continuing stream of interested local folk milling around to see the first steamers on this line for seven years, even though they were not in steam.

The only hitch now was that Sunter's big transporter had been delayed on its journey from South Wales, but Peter Sunter had arrived from his home at Northallerton to supervise. The route had been surveyed, the traffic police had been alerted and all due precautions and preparations made. But there remained one worry other than the overdue road transporter. It was whether or not 70013 would clear the railway bridge over the main road, at right angles to the sloping station approach. This corner was tight for such a long load, but the bridge headroom was only 16 feet above the road beneath. With *Oliver* standing thirteen-six, it allowed very little for the platform height of the huge eight-axled, 64 wheeled trailer. If a jam occurred between loco and bridge it would be far worse than the 12 mile detour which was the only alternative to the direct route under the bridge. According to measurements already taken, it would be touch and go, but Peter Sunter and I made further checks using a long spline of wood borrowed from the nearby timber merchant. We found that the road level varied by up to four inches under the bridge and keeping to where greatest headroom could be obtained would restrict the turn still more. *Thundersley* was to be loaded first and, by the time the 45 feet ramp up to the transporter had been built with timbers and rails, the day was too far gone to make the slow journey to Bressingham. Another of Sunter's lorries had brought the timber baulks, some so hefty that they had to be craned into position. Heavy rain had begun to fall again before the ramp was finished and the long day ended with both locos still on BR rails. But early next morning the haul began in sunshine. The winch on the haulage tractor began pulling at a snail's pace. Inch by inch it rose up the long ramp, but the angle between its rise and the level platform brought a worry as *Thundersley*'s front bogey wheel dangled above the rail. The first driving wheel to reach the platform top put more weight forward to bring the bogey wheels down but then came the reverse process when the rear bogey took off, along with the rear driving wheel till, at last, after an hour's slow rise, all wheels were levelled off on the trailer top rails to be chained and wire-roped for stability and security.

Thundersley's overall height was not in conflict with the bridge underpass, but the long process of loading was the same when it came to unload. We had tried to work in with the traffic police but if their timing requests were impossible to meet they did not complain and were always on call when crucial periods came. The most crucial was when, with *Oliver* aboard the trailer, its tractor took it, shorn of its tender, gingerly down to the main road where traffic had to be held up once the sharp turn was negotiated for the bridge. Some men had scrambled up the steep embankment with cameras, maybe hopeful of a unique startling shot of a locomotive stuck under a railway bridge. Bill Harvey was up there too with no such hopes, but on watchful duty eyeing things on the same level as *Oliver*'s squat chimney. A Sunter's man stood in front of the smokebox ready to shout if it failed to pass beneath the first bridge girder it came to at a dead slow pace. The shout came and the load shuddered to a stop. It would not clear by two or three inches. Peter Sunter climbed up to see for himself and then gave the order to let as much air from the trailer tyres as he dared. "It's risky", he whispered to me, "but it's worth it – and we should just make it. I'd hoped it would be enough to let the platform down as far as it will go." His men acted swiftly on all 64 wheels all on turning axles, whilst the police eased road traffic through a single narrow passage. Half an hour later the load nudged forward again and, as *Oliver*'s chimney emerged from beneath the other main girder, Peter grinned and whistled, "Phew! – if they'd given it another coat of paint we wouldn't have cleared it."

With its tender having to come on another load, *Oliver*'s cab was a gaping space at the rear. It was also the obvious place on which to ride the three miles to Bressingham for Robert, Adrian and myself. Not for prideful publicity, but for the sheer joy and excitement as we waved to people lining the road all the way. Boys ran alongside, little children stood awestruck, dogs barked and a police car rode ahead to warn of our approach. Secretly I wished for some means to do this by blowing the loco's whistle but only steam or compressed air would set off its musical tone. I'd also hoped to see a TV camera to record the event, which would have boosted open day receipts, but Anglia TV was banned by a technicians' strike and BBC, I learned later, did not come because their cameramen could find no film.

It was not with pride of either achievement or ownership that I found myself in such a favoured position as we moved sedately towards Diss town and Bressingham. Fulfilment of an airy dream begun long before, yes, but there was nothing but an awareness of my good fortune. And to be there with my two sons who had shared the hard times uncomplainingly with me engendered pride of a special kind. They could scarcely share to the full my enthusiasm for steam, but we were all of the same mind in our attachment to Bressingham, now to be enhanced by the guardianship of these noble locomotives.

The driver stopped now and then to let other Saturday holiday traffic through, but some of the cars behind us were obviously intent on seeing the process of unloading. As we reached the wooded S-bend at Roydon where the road slopes down to Bressingham, with our land on either side, a sudden flash-back came as a reminder of March 1950. Then, on a borrowed bike, I had coasted down the slope for the first time after having been absent in Canada for most of two years. I was nearly broke financially and, with nothing but hope that what I'd foolishly left behind was not beyond my ability to rescue and restore, thankful that all was not lost. On the same day I'd come across what was left of *Bella*, my first steam engine, to cause instant anger for such senseless destruction. On that sad, but deservedly chastening visit, I was alone because, with the house having been let to tenants and the secrecy of my return to jump on those who had failed in the trust placed in them, we had no home to return to at once. Now, it was all so different that I could wish the rest of my family were up with me on the footplate, so high above the road that the pattern of nursery fields was like a carpet, with the farmhouse nestling in the trees beyond.

That chastening experience had been an indication of an inherent flaw in my nature – of acting on impulse, so much as to blinker wiser considerations. Perhaps my venture into collecting steam engines was another example of what might be termed a subimatory motivation. But this time the first impulse had led on to firmer ground, and mixture though it was of self-expression and altruism, I had no doubts whatever on the score of worthiness, knowing that the concept of a live steam museum held considerable scope for further development. Truly the years since 1950 had dealt kindly with me, more so maybe than I deserved or could have hoped for. Small wonder then that I could look behind and wave to Jenny, Anthea and Flora in the first of the line of cars – and to Bridget who had returned specially from London for the great event of that weekend.

Oliver Cromwell *easing under Diss railway bridge with ½" to spare.*

Oliver Cromwell *arrives at Bressingham.*

Bubbling gently . . . as steam pressure rises.

CHAPTER TEN

OLIVER RIDES AGAIN

Oliver Cromwell, without the tender, was 40 tons heavier than *Thundersley*. Its only hand brake worked on the tender's wheels and for safe unloading, having gravity to contend with, called for extreme precautions. By the time the unloading ramp was built up on the Sunday morning the day's visitors were coming in and the possibility of up to 3,000 people standing or milling around held dangers to be strenuously avoided. Nothing must be left to chance and both *Bertha* and *Black Prince* were in steam ready to take whatever strain was needed on their respective winch ropes. The winch on the road transporter had pulled each locomotive onto the trailer platform but now it served to keep a tight rope, gradually easing as Arthur Prentice on *Bertha* pulled in until *Oliver*'s main weight was on the down sloping ramp. Such a weight against the pull of gravity made us keep the crowd well back, for a snapped steel cable could be lethal. A wire rope doesn't just fall limp when broken but jumps and lashes, one never knows where. Arthur's winding in as the transporter's winch was released did not work well because of differing speed ratios and was sometimes in opposition to one another making for greater risk of a cable snapping. Fears rose as *Oliver*'s front wheels settled down on to our rails, leaving the rear six drivers suspended over the angle where the ramp rails met them. *Bertha*'s cable twanged with tension and then snapped, with the jagged end snaking back like a live thing, leaving me on *Black Prince* to take the strain, thankful that both road engines had been used against such a happening and that no-one had been hurt.

With all 24 of *Oliver*'s wheels safely down onto our new laid tracks, I could relax and did so by sitting on the driver's seat in the cab, contentedly smoking my pipe, watching the crowd and the final move. This was for the transporter which had of course straddled the track to move away once the ramp was cleared. Behind it, close to the door of the big shed, stood *Oliver*'s tender and it would be my job to pull it up with *Black Prince* for coupling back to its proper place to make 70013 complete once more. The crowd had gone. So many had stood around to watch and, although plans had been carefully laid to avoid a Sunday, weather and unexpected delays had contrived to make the unloading at the worst possible time. It was no greater an influx of visitors than usual, for there had been no advance publicity as I'd hoped and schemed for when planning a Friday arrival. Only two weeks before there were large crowds through the gate for what I believed had to be the last Steam Gala. We called it a gala rather than a rally because space was too restricted to invite more than just a few engines from outside to join in. Since then a railway cutting had been made in the little meadow to reduce traction engine space still more.

It was a popular enough event but the new dimension taking in full scale-locomotives brought new responsibilities and the work of organising the gala was such as to become a burden, which in future would be intolerable. But it was these events which had indirectly led to widening the scope and revenue from them was helping to pay the heavy cost of bringing the big locomotives to Bressingham.

Thankfully two reasonably fine days for the Steam Gala on the first weekend of August brought in around 8,000 people each day but the rainy pattern continued. Harvesting was nigh on a mockery, and iron-wheeled traction engines at the gala had churned up the paddocks to make subsequent parking a problem. Notwithstanding the willingness of those able to help, from Robert to Mary Fox, the firm's secretary, a red light was beginning to glimmer for me as overall responsibilities increased – and were likely to become still greater. The steam side, along with the twice-weekly public openings were becoming almost a business on its own and the need for a manager was becoming apparent. With some relief from the extra pressure of the past few weeks there was no need to dread the function booked for Saturday 14 September. It was to be host to a plenary meeting of the Association of Railway Preservation Societies to be chaired by Captain Peter Manisty. About 90 delegates turned up and, though dull and cold, we were able to give steam rides before providing refreshments during the course of the formal meeting. This took place inside the new shed in the space which had been planned for the 14 road using engines, until now having to be outside covered with tilts.

It was a change as well as a pleasure to meet others interested or involved with steam preservation and, for the first time, given a clear insight into the work done by the Association under the energetic chairmanship of Peter Manisty. For the delegates it was a change to come where no railway had ever been and, if the new shed was little more than half full, *Oliver Cromwell*'s splendid bulk was proof that preservation was not unworthily served in what had been a farmyard. I was conscious that some purist enthusiasts were unlikely to see it that way and a remark made by one such who buttonholed me, with an expression which betrayed his own feelings – "A lion in a budgie cage," is what I heard somebody say. It was also said that BR would be rapped for letting such locos as the Britannia come to a "Norfolk cabbage patch." "Just what's being said, mind you, but I thought you ought to know." And he turned away. With the meeting over, I repeated what the young man had said, to Peter Manisty. "Sour grapes, eh?" he commented, "but I know of no other place where I could feel so confident that they will be well cared for. And if you've a mind to take in one or two more you can count on me backing you up with the Panel and John Scholes." This made me blink. Not that such a hope was absent from my mind but I did not wish to push my luck too far, too fast.

Reading my expression perhaps, Peter suggested the Stanier-built tank, No 2500, also needed a good home. "And", he added, "it would complement *Thundersley* there – with room to place it on the same track. I expect you know it was the first of a new class to supersede the *Thundersley* type on the London, Tilbury and Southend in the 1930s. All 37 of them were 2–6–4 tanks with three cylinders giving a quick getaway on heavy commuter trains, and 2500 has been in store for several years at Brighton, Preston Park. Think it over."

"I don't need to," came my glib reply, with eyes lighting up.

"Good! Then what about putting in for the J.17 as well? It's also at Brighton, but as the last loco to run in East Anglia and based at Norwich, it's a good candidate for Bressingham surely?"

I had, however, a peculiar reservation over this class. The

0–6–0 engine with inside cylinders had been something of a bogey for me as a small child. So often I'd had nightmares of being fixed between the tracks unable to escape as one of them came charging towards me. Beneath its front buffer beam there were two rods moving in and out with inexorable regularity and waking up just as it reached me left me breathless with fright. Now, 60 years later, those memories came back so vividly that I had to explain my hesitation.

Peter laughed, with a hand on my shoulders. "Isn't it about time", he said, "to lay that old bogey? The J.17 has been restored – at least superficially – though it may not be a runner as I'm pretty sure 2500 is. I think they should both be here, and so far as I know neither has been applied for by any other concern. What do you say? I don't think you need make a formal application if I pass the word to John Scholes."

With more exciting prospects in mind, next morning I was up in good time to light up *Oliver Cromwell*. It was dull and chilly but it would be more than merely comforting to get a good fire going before breakfast. Being mid-September, maybe only a small crowd could be expected for the afternoon opening and maybe the sun would shine. In two weeks we would be closing down until next Easter with a vast amount of work to do both indoors and out. Overnight a tractor-operated winch had been placed in position with which to draw 70013 out into the open for firing to avoid filling the shed with smoke. With one helper to man the tractor, it was my privilege to stand ready to apply the tender hand brake once clear of the shed. I'd piled two barrow loads of wood onto the footplate, along with dry kindling and oily rags the evening before. BR practice had been to toss coal around a firelighter placed in the box and leave it for an hour or two before throwing in more coal. There was obviously good reason to apply heat slowly to avoid over-rapid metal expansion, but it seemed to me that under BR practice the metal scarcely began to warm at all for the first hour or two, and to take four hours as I expected to do, would cause no harm. Six or seven hours was being over-cautious.

Oily rags on the shovel soon caught fire with a match and reaching well into the huge firebox – of 42 square feet of space over the firebars – I let the rags fall near the centre, when well alight. Next the kindling and with this too flaming, larger lumps and lengths of wood followed. Smoke was lazily coming out of the far away chimney but, in spite of the firehole door being shut, it was escaping back into the cab as well. Five minutes worth of clean air at the window to allow the wood fire to produce more flame and less smoke, then came the hardest task. Sliding back the firehole doors, the shovelling began, not with an ordinary shovel, but one with a short handle and a large capacity mouth. With coal smoke now belching back into the cab, I counted each throw, trying to spread it evenly all over. There was no escaping that smoke, though by keeping head well down, my lung intake was somewhat less. Fifty eight, fifty nine, sixty I counted and, clanging the firedoor closed rushed for the open footplate door, gasping, but with a subdued sense of achievement. I prided myself on knowing something about fire-lighting from stoves to bush or bonfire and traction engines could be included, but never before had I lit and stoked one like this – a firebox in which 10 men could stand.

Oliver Cromwell was beginning to make steam two hours later when George Ewles arrived to take over. He had recently retired as an express train driver at Norwich and had gladly volunteered to drive at Bressingham now that permission had been given for footplate riding on our short track, provided a qualified driver was in charge.

"It's like greeting an old friend," he said as he walked around 70013. "Many's the time I've come through Diss station at 90 with this or another of the Britannias we had. I had four or five years on the diesels since steam finished but I'm a steam man. Steam in the blood I reckon, and I'm hully glad to have the chance to drive again, that I am. And now I must take the oil can round. But what's the weather going to do?"

The weather was not promising. It was still dull, like a grey blanket over the whole sky. Rain began to fall soon after noon, lightly at first, but an hour later it was so heavy that after one round on the Nursery Line *George Sholto* was put away, leaving only me with *Gwynedd* waiting to see if any passengers wished to ride in the uncovered coaches. But none of the handful of visitors was that keen and they were all under the cover of the locomotive shed. I too had to take shelter from the pitiless rain. When measured next morning, after persisting all night, 4.38 inches was the most ever over the 40 odd years I'd been re-

From inside the firebox of an express locomotive, showing the fire-hole door and stay rivets.

cording for a 24 hour period. It spelled trouble. Through our narrow valley had to pass all surplus rainfall from an area of about 30,000 acres. On every acre 438 tons thereabouts of water had fallen on land already saturated by previous rains. Fears of flooding were well-founded. Within hours, the low places on the Fen were under water which spread out quickly until almost all lay submerged. But that was not all.

It may be considered irrelevant to describe happenings which had no direct connection with steam engines but the latter had come and were still coming to a rural site well away from their normal habitat and as a background both geographical and economic could but be influential in the success or failure as a comprehensive live museum. The downpour itself made virtually no difference. Parts of the narrow gauge track were flooded and washouts of ballast had to be made good. From the standpoint of the farm and nursery business which formed, indirectly but unavoidably, the economic or financial background, it was a disaster. Two fields containing half a million plants in wide variety had been a delight as much for me as for the passengers in my little train but after being submerged for a week they were dead and stinking. The autumn season for lifting and despatching orders had just begun and now we had to let our customers down. Because many were not commonly grown for sale, it was poor consolation that these would not be bought elsewhere. Frames holding over 200,000 cuttings were also drowned, and in places water had rushed down sandy slopes and erosion had exposed the roots of some plants whilst covering others in silt. Such a flood had been feared for years. Pleas to the Drainage Authority to which we paid rates to improve the bottlenecked River Waveney had been largely ignored. Now they might as well act, but such damage had been done that 1968 would be a loss-making year and plans for a large new building for the nursery had to be postponed, along with changes of priority affecting my own plans for improving visitor amenities and other developments for the steam museum, since it could be no other but tenant of the nursery and farm property.

It was some compensation when, after a week, the narrow gauge was again operational, also to bring *Oliver Cromwell* back to life for the last but one open Sunday of the season. The lighting up formula was repeated and again George Ewles arrived just as the pressure gauge needle was lifting. Again he stood back admiringly before climbing up nimbly to the footplate. Checking the pressure, he then opened the blower valve which sent steam up the chimney to draw up the sluggish fire, sending smoke high into the air. An hour later, having oiled round, he gave a hoot on the whistle and opened the regulator. Out came jets of steam from the cylinder relief valves with such force and volume that gave some notice of the immense impact live steam made on the piston head. Then the wheels began to turn as the piston rods took the thrust, with steam jets still shooting and noisily hissing far out in front as the valves did their job. Only gentle puffs came from the chimney. This first operation, as the great engine came to life, was an arresting, almost awesome moment for me, and one better viewed and appreciated standing close by to watch rather than to be up there on the footplate. Flora stood there also watching, awestruck. Satisfied that all was well, George beckoned us up and with some reluctance Flora fell to his and my persuasion, but she confessed to being rather scared. *Oliver* was allowed to glide back down the gradient to the lower end of the line and then, in forward gear, George opened up to take us the full length of the short, makeshift track, with a hoot and a sharply forceful exhaust from the chimney. It was Flora's first footplate experience and, in spite of it being a thrill, as she said, it was one she would not be keen to repeat.

Footplate riding for visitors had for me become an important if not vital part of the whole aspect of live steam. We had no preserved length of redundant railway as had other centres where steam preservation was a public show. Many other centres were following the example set by the Bluebell Railway, which showed that what BR under Beeching discarded as uneconomic could be self-supporting because of the widespread nostalgia for steam, with volunteer helpers obtaining their kicks thereby. But here, with only 300 yards of track, to pull coaches for passengers would have been quite ridiculous and yet, by giving footplate rides with such as George Ewles as both driver and commentator on the magic and power of steam, it could be a feature in keeping with the whole set-up, and one scarcely to be experienced where steam trains operated on a preserved section of ex-BR line. Although the public response to this was positive enough, snags had already appeared. One was that a crossing place which people had to use between the steam area and the garden would have to be manned as a danger point. The other was that the track was too short, as well as too fraught for people to savour fully the experience and thrill. This was my belief and concern and for a time I toyed with this notion for lack of alternative in extending forwards. This would have entailed continuing the tight bend in the paddock, just missing the private drive to my house, to cross the main nursery roadway and run close to and parallel with the main road. Expounding the idea to Robert, he was quick to point out what I already feared, that, apart from another dangerous crossing, the Highway Authority would ban such a menace to passing traffic, distracting as it would be to drivers.

There was no lack of other distractions than this for me that autumn and winter. The handsome 2–6–4 Stanier Tank No 2500 was safely housed before the year ended. It was followed by the plain but sturdy 0–6–0 J.17 and in taking a close look at the motion, with its piston rod extensions which featured so frighteningly in my childhood nightmares, any remaining bogey was firmly laid. Both were in need of repainting and Don Hubbard, now on the permanent staff, took on the tedious task of scraping down 2500, with his usual quiet zeal before tackling the more rewarding application of primer and coat after coat of black paint. There could be no choice of any other colour than that of its original. This was the unquestioned rule for any locomotive coming under our care as a historical relic on permanent loan. But when another industrial was offered by Peter Bland, having purchased it from the Beckton Gas Works, we agreed that a deep red would be distinctive livery since its original colour was so faded as to be unsure of what it was. This Beckton Works No 1 was also a squat 0–4–0. Having a side instead of a saddle tank as had No 25 from the same works, it had outside cylinders, and though built by Neilson in 1892 it was relatively modern in overall appearance. A steam test proved that it was still a runner. Also in consultation with Jim Price, presenter of *William Francis*, a brown was chosen instead of its original black. He had some helpers and scraped and painted but the top coat had been faulty – a paint which failed to be what it was supposed to be – and a new brand was used to give it the livery of the defunct Midland and Great Northern Joint Railway, based at Melton Constable, north of Norwich.

In no more than a year since the big shed was completed, seven standard gauge locomotives had arrived. Such an influx would have exceeded all expectations. But then, the whole concept had been something of a gamble to begin with, based mainly on the knowledge that if I'd not taken the plunge in building the shed, there would have been no engines offered in order to fill it. It was not, however, full, even with the traction engines ranged on one side, nor had it a hard floor where there were no railway tracks, but somewhat loose gravelly hoggin which needed to be sprayed with water to lay the dust before visitors arrived. Some day the cost of a concrete and asphalt floor would have to be afforded but it was not in my nature to spend money in advance of necessity when making shift allowed some freedom to acquire more exhibits which might come unexpectedly on offer.

A Norwegian 2–6–0 did come on offer to become the next arrival and, although we paid the cost of shipment, Gerald Pagano retained his ownership. As a steam enthusiast with a Norwegian wife, he had bought this quite good looking Swedish built engine but had nowhere to store and steam it, following the repaint he wished to do on his own. In the belief that given the facilities he asked for, the loco would stay at Bressingham, a verbal agreement was swiftly reached. Every weekend Gerald laboured scraping down and repainting. The task took him a year in spite of driving himself as if his life depended on finishing it. When it emerged into the open in the light apple green colour he had chosen, Gerald was obviously a very proud man as he affixed a nameplate he'd had made. It was named *King Haakon VII* because it was believed to be the locomotive which took His Majesty to Narvik or wherever it was he transferred to a British ship bound for England as the Nazis invaded Norway. With steam up at Bressingham, Gerald enjoyed chuffing up and down on his own on a non-open day, and it was then that I realised this was what he wanted to repeat – and on open days too maybe – whenever he felt so inclined. Misgivings on the part of both my regular helpers and me intervened, and warnings on safety grounds had to be made. Gerald took a certain umbrage and in quite a short space of time *King Haakon* was no longer part of the Bressingham scene.

Geoff Sands had by this time come to Bressingham as Chief Mechanical Engineer. After nearly 30 years, starting from the bottom at Norwich, he had climbed the BR ladder to become Locomotive Shed Master at Crewe North where I first met him following the introduction made by his father who had been the Inspector accompanying me on my first express footplate ride in 1961. Transferring to Salisbury MPD and then to Basingstoke as steam was killed off, he became unsettled just at the time when I felt the need of expert help and advice was an overriding necessity. Now, at a much-reduced salary, he said he was back in his element and it soon became clear that what he did not know about steam locomotives, inside and out, was scarcely worth knowing. Jack and Roger had been an utterly reliable pair so far, but their sphere of experience was soundly based on road- using engines. They had done splendid work in restoring these at Bressingham and had taken enthusiastically to narrow-gauge locomotives. Although all steam engines built on the reciprocating motion principles powered by cylinder, valves and piston under steam pressure, the much larger railway locomotives were too much for them to cope with as additional to those already under their skill and care.

It was Geoff who went down to Dagenham docks, owned by Samuel Williams & Co, to supervise the loading of Gerald Pagano's Norwegian engine for road transportation. When he returned he reported the existence of a Manning Wardle industrial locomotive on a plinth just inside the dock gates. Further information was that it had become shabby from exposure and that the directors were of a mind to ensure preservation of what had been a favourite in their fleet, by allowing it to come to Bressingham. In due course the 1877, 28 ton 0–6–0 bearing its original name *Solomon* arrived to occupy a little more of the unused space of the shed which we now considered was worthy of a large notice board stating 'Bressingham Steam Museum'.

Perhaps it was the peculiar charm I saw in the Norwegian *King Haakon* – along with some regrets that it was no longer with us – which prompted me to look into the possibility of another of Continental design. There was something to be said for obtaining one to show visitors what differences there were between them and British – or what developments foreigners had made to the basic British invention. With this in mind when on a trip to North Germany, I went to Hamburg to be shown round the DBB depot there. Steam was giving way to diesel and electricity but, unlike BR, it was with less haste and locomotives came out of service only when they were thereabouts life expired or in need of major repair and replacement. None of the latter, it appeared, was for sale which was perhaps just as well, and I was advised to travel up to Denmark. Not that I was in a position to

King Haakon VII, *Swedish built from Norway.*

do a deal, but just to look around and decide what might be available as a worthwhile acquisition, and what costs would be to import one. At Frederica a collection of redundant locomotives was decidedly interesting. There were 4–6–2 Pacifics, 2–10–0 freight engines and a few much smaller, much older types which, as a collection, covered a period of 80 years of mainly Swedish design.

It was strange being there in Denmark with an object so different to when I was last there in 1953. Then it was entirely nurseries and what they produced, but now I had no thought for them. It was a temptation to go on to Norway as I had done in 1953, which included a journey behind one of the magnificent NSB mountain locomotives – which might now be redundant. But on learning that a Danish Pacific would probably cost more to transport to England than the £3,000 – reasonable enough – for the purchase price, there was nothing for it but to make for Esbjerg and back to England myself in frustrated acceptance of what could not be. At least, not yet.

LMS no. 2500 *from the National Collection.*

Royal Scot.

CHAPTER ELEVEN

LIONS IN THE BUDGIE CAGE

There was plenty to keep us all occupied for a year or two at least without any more engines coming under our charge, whether British or foreign. On open days most of the now permanent staff of nine, including two part-timers, were needed to meet the visitors' demands. This did not, incidentally, include catering, this being a franchise for a local firm, along with ice-cream vans, sweets and cigarettes, fruit and so on, as well as stalls for fund-raising charities. Drivers, firemen and general dogsbodies were all fully employed for the few hectic open hours twice weekly. To open every day or more often than about 50 times a year would have been uneconomical with six or seven engines gobbling up coal. In between openings there was maintenance as well as restoration work going on, but what stood out starkly was the need for a longer, safer track on which to give footplate rides. The increasing number of visitors was fine for contributing to expenses, but where they crossed *Oliver Cromwell*'s track was so fraught with danger that someone had to stand there with a rope to hold them back on the warning whistle.

The only possible way a different track length could be laid was in the opposite direction. It had to use the tree-girt Causeway lane which ran south serving the fen fields. It was not only narrow, with a deep ditch on the west side, but was humped as a causeway with no firm surface over the peaty soil beneath. To ballast it for a railway safe enough for a heavy locomotive would have been not only costly but would have made it unusable for any other vehicle and tractors which often had to use it. It was simply not wide enough for both. The bordering trees of oak, poplar, ash and alder were quite large and to fell them would be close to sacrilege. Then one day, with spade in hand, I dug a little hole into rutty track to see what, if any, road-making material might have been strewn there before my time. There was nothing but a sandy mixture of soil, doubtless put there by whoever dug the bordering ditch long ago. But there were tree roots – lots of them – a few inches below, and this brought a possible answer to the problem.

A few days later, in response to a telephone call, a BR permanent way expert was saying that in such circumstances tree roots would indeed form a safer base for a railway track than ballast. This was good news. All we needed to do was to let in each sleeper onto a few inches of sand, and waste sand from the nursery was waiting for somewhere to dump it. This would induce the trees to seek it and make for a living mat of roots, and with the same mixture filled in over the sleepers up to rail top level it could still be used as a roadway. Sand could also be dug here and there not far away from low banks from centuries of upland erosion into the valley. It packed down firmly mixed with soil, as I'd found when laying narrow gauge track formation. So here was an easy, inexpensive answer. Although a four feet high embankment had to be made to ease the gradient from the end of the existing track down to the Causeway, this was no great problem. By the time autumn rains came to turn workable material to mud, the new formation was complete except for the rail itself. Its 600 yard length stopped short of the by-pass river, a bridge over which would not be worth the cost since, beyond, the terrain was quite boggy. Then came a lucky find of a redundant works siding near Bury St Edmunds, there, almost for the taking as far as cost was concerned, were enough rail and sleepers to finish it off.

With the open season at an end, Geoff took a rambling holiday with just a hint that he might call in to see an old friend at Skegness in the shape of *Royal Scot*. But I knew well enough that it meant more than merely renewing his acquaintance with that famous LMS locomotive which he himself had driven in his time on a testing run after an overhaul. He came back with the news that, mainly due to the salty air at Butlin's Holiday Camp where it was on static display as an attraction, it was in a rapidly deteriorating condition. Sir Billy Butlin had placed two locomotives at each of four holiday camps and no doubt they had been something of a draw. That was in 1962, but it was doubtful if he had foreseen either the effect of salty winds or of the vandalism which had caused the Skegness manager to tell Geoff that they had become nothing but a tiresome nuisance.

'Duchess of Sutherland', *ex Butlins Holiday Camp at Ayr, restricted to life at Bressingham.*

The Brighton Terrier 'Martello' *at 1875 is the oldest loco at Bressingham.*

"I'd dearly love to see it here," Geoff said with feeling. "And there's the London and South Western shunter standing beside it." To this I heartily agreed but had to express doubts, having already written an appeal three years before on learning that they were suffering. The reply from Butlin's Head Office had been rather frosty. Making no reference to this occasion, I wrote again and the result was a visit from one of the directors early in November. Having seen what there was to show him by way of supporting emphasis he took us by surprise by as good as saying we could have the lot, all eight, located at Minehead, Pwllheli and Ayr as well as Skegness. So long as we paid for transport and restoration they could stay at Bressingham on permanent loan.

At first elation took over. Such a prospect was almost unbearable in its magnitude and the boost it would be for us, with the addition of two Duchess Pacifics, a Princess Class, as well as *Royal Scot* and four smaller locomotives. But it wasn't long before we came down to earth. We had neither shed space nor other resources – funds, labour and workshop facilities for more than four.

"Well then", the Butlin's Director said cheerily, "just take your pick."

It was, however, to be a restrictive selection. The Director had overlooked the fact that those at Minehead and Pwllheli were featured in the next year's Butlin's brochure and would have to be ruled out for fear of offence under the Trades Descriptions Act. We had also overlooked a factor constituting another snag. It was that at least one other railway preservation centre had made a previous application, of which our Director friend was unaware. Their letter or whatever had been shelved but news of the impending dispersal of the locomotives was bound to reach them and possibly thwart any plans we made.

As quickly and quietly as possible we alerted Sunters and, on David Ward's advice, the BR shed master at Ayr. From there the 4–6–2 *Duchess of Sutherland* would have to be rail-hauled to Norfolk but *Royal Scot* would come by road, as would the little Brighton Terrier and the LSW shunter. The news leaked out and for several weeks it was touch and go whilst the complicated preparations were made. There were vociferous protests from enthusiasts who believed the locos should go where there was mainline access and who saw Bressingham more as a prison for them. Others protested that they had a prior claim but thankfully for us Butlins insisted that theirs was the right to place their locomotives where and with whom they chose. News that *Royal Scot* was on its way from Skegness was comforting. When it arrived with the tender on a separate low loader, it had travelled about 150 miles although Skegness was well under 100 miles distant as the crow flies. It had been routed by police and highway authorities to avoid traffic congestion as well as low rail bridges and others considered unsafe for its 110 ton weight.

Duchess of Sutherland, however, was given the rare distinction of being towed by a diesel loco on BR lines without having the connecting rods removed. This procedure for locomotives on tow was in force because in the past axle boxes and big ends had heated to cause delay and damage. But Bill Bennett at Ayr MPD had made extra precautions, whilst Bill Harvey and Geoff Sands undertook to travel as the experts to prevent trouble on the way. The 164 ton *Duchess* was shunted into a siding at Norwich for safety's sake, none the worse for its 400 mile journey, adorned with a long banner proclaiming its ownership and destination. Its arrival caused considerable local interest as had *Oliver Cromwell* but for me it was of a special kind as we viewed it that day – until that is, the telephone woke me that night at well past midnight. It was from a solicitor acting on behalf of another party who, he said, had a prior claim. He had obtained a legal injunction to prevent the loco from being moved. By morning another call came announcing that the injunction had been affixed to its cabside and was not to be removed pending a court hearing. The thought of a legal battle caused many hours' loss of sleep. But after a week of anxiety the judge at Leeds Crown Court simply dismissed the case saying that the claim had no legal substance. Butlins had easily proved right of disposal, leaving the plaintiffs with no case to pursue. One could not help feeling sorry for that little group of young enthusiasts on learning that they had been duped by an older, unscrupulous man who had incited them to take legal action in the belief that the *Duchess of Sutherland* could thereby be diverted to their own railway preservation centre.

When at last the anxious week ended, all four of the Butlin locomotives were safely let down on rails again, with the enor-

Sir David Follett in the cab of Royal Scot.

mity of the task ahead becoming fully apparent. Their appearance was indeed shabby but it was easy enough to see which side of each had been exposed to the salty winds. Nothing short of the full treatment of scraping down and using filler paste where rust had eaten in to leave pock marks would suffice. When making some effort to calculate what restoration costs would be, budgeting for funds likely to be available, I had been obviously over-optimistic in putting *Royal Scot* at £3,000 and the *Duchess* at £5,000 for exterior work. This, I felt, had to be the priority, to effectively halt the further penetration of rust. Internally they were bound to incur costs as well, and visitor appeal had to be considered. Don Hubbard gave them many a wry look, knowing that to bring them back to a smart appearance whilst applying his own high standards of thoroughness he reckoned he had three years' work even with someone to help with the rough jobs. At the time they arrived he was stuck underneath the tender of *Oliver Cromwell*. This had not been tackled when having its overhaul at Crewe and to scrape out every nook and cranny as well as the plainer metal bottom, lying or crouching to work above his head, was both tedious and dirty.

For Geoff the prospect of coping with four more engines was very different. His concern was to have the two LMS express engines in running order again. His approach was much more intimate – like that of a doctor towards patients he'd known for years, coming under his care in dire straits. His diagnosis came with meticulous care to examine every part under suspicion as likely to need a remedy. Once I saw him give one of them a little loving pat – and the expression on his face was telling them to be patient. He was as good as saying, "It'll be all right, my beauties. Give me time and I'll give you back your pride." Understandable, for Geoff had been at Crewe when both the *Scot* and the *Duchess* were being prepared for purchase by Sir Billy Butlin to go on show at his holiday camps.

Between us we decided on priorities. *Royal Scot* must come first and then the *Duchess of Sutherland* and a year thereabouts was allowed for each. The two smaller ones would have to wait and, in any case, their exterior condition was less rough. The 0–6–0 so-called 'Brighton Terrier' bore the name *Martello* and, built as it was in 1875, was now doyen of the collection. As a class they had a long life in service on the London, Brighton and

South Coast Railway, some having topped 80 years. The 40 ton 1903 London and South Western Railways shunter, named *Granville* had only two sets of wheels as an 0–4–0, with large outside cylinders for the power needed when shunting stock around the Ocean Terminal at Southampton. This we decided must stay outside for the present for now all indoor space was taken and occupied. We had in fact laid a fourth track in the shed in anticipation of the influx and the metre gauge *Banshee*, never fitting in with the rest, had to go. It was sold to a steam centre at Embsay, Yorkshire. There was also *Joyce* outside. This was a totally enclosed Sentinel which was more like a diesel than a steamer in appearance and we'd been requested to give it a home by the Industrial Railway Society.

All-out concentration on *Royal Scot* involved much more than scraping away rust and applying preservative paint. Geoff decided that the three cylinders – two outside and one inside might well have rusty rings or valve surfaces and, for the same reason, the whole motion was taken apart as well as all cab fittings and injectors, each part being labelled for re-assembly. There were three sets of tubes in the boiler to be examined. The scores of small tubes seemed to be in fair condition, but not so the multiple sets of super-heater elements within the large flue tubes, 4½ inches in diameter. To take these out for inspection or replacement involved removal of the heavy super- heater header inside the smoke box and, as the boiler thus became disembowelled, so faults were calculated and segregated either for mending or renewal. A great accumulation had to be dealt with methodically. The eastern bay of the shed had now become the workshop with benches and machine tools moved over from the makeshift one near the old barn which was given over to spares and other reserved equipment, such as brake blocks and tubes. Staff had been slowly but steadily increased, not so much in keeping with additional work to be done, but more rigorously with funds available for wages. I had never been other than a volunteer and had perforce gradually to spend less time on engines and more on my nursery and garden work. Robert and Adrian had become joint managing directors of the family business which they were fast expanding. Amongst the regular staff was Philip Gray. He had come at weekends and holidays for years whilst still a schoolboy and now was keen to become a craftsman-mechanic, learning as fast as he could from such experts as Jack, Roger and Geoff. They taught him not only special steam skills and mechanics, but method as well. Jack and Roger had for years shown a reluctance to have several mechanical repair or removal jobs going at the same time. Two engines if need be, they said, but no more than two, with bits and pieces lying about which might get mixed up or mislaid. Two were all right because if one gets held up for some new part or for George Garrard to come for a special welding job, then a switch can be made from one to the other. Geoff took the same view but, although this working practice did not apply to exteriors such as scraping and painting, there had to be coordination so that one type of operation did not impinge on or impede another.

One worrying hold-up occurred just as the final re-assembly was taking place on *Royal Scot*. It had been planted with us by an ex-BR fitter at Nottingham Shed, where *Royal Scot* was last in use in 1962. He told us that the reason for its being withdrawn from service was a fracture in the main steam J pipe which took the super-heated steam from the boiler to the dome and so to the cylinders. If this were true, and we were assured it was, then the pipe had to be renewed or put to rights. Tests of several kinds, including electronic, were made with the boiler cleared out, but no fracture showed up. It was puzzling and very worrying, but in the end Geoff decided it could only have been a leaky joint. Yet there was the lingering fear that, when all other boiler work had been renewed or replaced, then the hidden fault would again become evident when under full steam. This would have been disastrous because the large element flues had all been re-threaded on renewed ends 18 inches long, welded on at over £19 each.

Geoff's hunch was correct. The man from Nottingham could not have known the exact cause of the trouble because no inside examination of the boiler could have been undertaken at the time of withdrawal from service without disembowelling it as we had done. He had, it seemed, jumped to the conclusion that the J pipe was fractured, for both water and steam tests at extra pressure proved successful. In its splendid maroon livery, lettered and lined out by Bob Rolfe, a local craftsman, *Royal Scot* went into service on open days that summer, a delight to behold. But it had cost over £10,000 to bring it back once more to life and splendour.

As with *Royal Scot*, so with *Duchess of Sutherland*. Her boiler tubes were in better condition but her firebox was not. This huge orifice, almost deep enough for standing upright had been made of inch thick copper. In places it was wasted to half an inch and in one a patch had to be inserted, as had several copper patch screws, all very expensively put in by two BR boilersmiths from Norwich. Bob Rolfe came again to give the final coat of maroon paint, to be followed by lining out but, being too impatient to see the *Duchess* in steam again, we did not wait for Bob – a master builder and versatile craftsman – to line her out with his delicate sable hair brushes. Pride and joy on that day were, however, mixed with sadness. The firebox had only been patched and the boiler inspector warned us that repairs were not only inadequate but that the whole of one side would need replacement before a full certificate could enable us to use it for footplate riding. Back in the shed, to become, we feared, a permanently static exhibit until or unless at least double the £15,000 restoration it had already cost could be found to remedy the firebox weakness.

Now that we had several locomotives with inside cylinders or valve gear or both, Geoff explained that an inspection pit was a vital necessity. He had also persuaded me that sooner or later we would need a wheel drop pit as well as a wheel lathe on which to renew worn tyre profiles. Both were very hefty pieces of equipment which we were able to procure from Carlisle and Upperby. No time had come yet in which to instal either, and now the inspection pit had to come first. The bay of the nearby Dutch barn was less used nowadays for straw storage and this was virtually commandeered with Robert as farm manager having no real objection. A long pit four feet deep and the width of the track was dug out, as were footings for walls on both sides of the 90 feet length. One of the hardest tasks for years came my way to barrow load after load of concrete to underpin the wall on the inside, separating one bay of the barn from the other, where empty sows lived under an upper floor filled with baled straw. The pit itself was put out to contract for concreting. The walls had to be heavily reinforced for on them, embedded, unsleepered rails would have to bear some very heavy weight. Another 'road', as enginemen called railway tracks, meant another set of points to join up with the centre running line. And by the time they were used to drive in *Thundersley* and the 2500 Tank, two more sets of points were being planned.

One of our regular visiting volunteers was Patrick Evendon, an executive for the British end of Renault cars. He was familiar with French railways too, and knew some high-up SNCF officials. He also knew that their American built 141 class was being phased out and suggested with no prompting from me that one would fit in with my deferred notion of adding a foreign loco to the collection. Negotiations undertaken by Patrick were protracted. Then after several months he told us that at Sarraguemines near Metz in Eastern France a batch of 141s was awaiting disposal and we could have our pick. Geoff and he went to do just that and then it was for Roger and Philip Gray to go over as guards on the locomotive as it was towed to Dunkirk for shipment to Harwich. Geoff and I went to Harwich to meet it, to find it emerging from below decks on rails, with Sunter's big transporter waiting on the quayside. It had been said that this class was at least partially designed by the French and in fact its appearance gave that impression. As a 2–8–2 it was impressive and I would not have been surprised if the given weight of 156 tons was an understatement. It had none of the sleekness of a British design but, as a general purpose loco – for both freight and passenger, it looked immensely powerful and, in a sense, formidable. The Americans and Canadians had built 1,300 of them with which to rehabilitate French railways after the Second World War, under the Marshall Plan. This one, No 73, had been built by Lima in Ohio in 1946 and, although so grimy that its original paint was scarcely visible, this we did not mind because repainting would have to wait.

Incidentally, it was rumoured that the Americans requested the return of one as a museum exhibit and, although the whole batch was by way of a gift from the US Government, the French wanted to charge them for it. Perhaps it was only the £3,000 they charged us, but the Americans jibbed and the loco selected for them was still standing on the dockside at Marseilles. At Bressingham more rails had been laid on which to place it whilst transport from Harwich had to be by road because its width was too great for BR station platforms, and its height too much for overhead bridges. This resulted in transport costs well above the purchase price. These restrictions applied also to our main loco shed and a third structure – of steel – was found second- hand and reasonably priced to give space 100 feet long with two more tracks inside just west of the main building and running line.

So now we had a foreign locomotive with both French and American features. An appropriate name occurred. Tom Paine was an Englishman, renegade though he also was. He was reared at nearby Thetford and spent much of his adult life in both America and France in the late 1700s when both countries were anti-British. At least Tom Paine was a purposeful revolutionary and some of the ideas he expressed in his book 'The Rights of Man' in time became accepted by the land of his birth.

Long before this example of foreign steam development arrived, a very different one had been located and was the cause of many a letter and telephone call. News had come over the grapevine that in Norway five German Class 52 2–10–0s had been literally unearthed. They had been sent to Norway from Germany when new during the war, for service under Nazi occupation. After the capitulation, NSB took possession and for a few years used them as freight engines. Then five were placed under NATO ownership. After overhauling them they were sealed up in a disused tunnel near Sandnes as strategic reserves and there they remained for 14 years. A local ex-engine driver turned scrap dealer knew of their existence and his offer to purchase them was finally accepted. On examination, three, he reckoned, were ruined by water dripping from the tunnel roof but two, though red with rust, were not beyond rescue. A letter from me led to an English-speaking Norwegian enthusiast acting go-between and a deal was done – for another £3,000. After that followed more than a year of frustrating delays.

Having been warned that, in the absence of a rail ferry, the cost of craneage onto a ship would probably exceed £1,000, I wrote letters to Danish, German and Belgian railways hoping that it could be hauled round to a Channel ferry port. None of these systems was interested. Back to a Norwegian shipping firm and a quote of £7,000 was made – exclusive of crane hire – which would be also a charge at an east coast port of entry – and left me feeling pretty helpless. Then my Norwegian contact gave the news of a small ship sometimes calling at Stavanger which was specially built for heavy indivisible loads as it had its own cranes aboard. It had recently left for Africa but he would keep track of it through the vessel's agent and let me know when it was likely to be available for cargo in Norway. Months later a phone call came from the agent. The *Stokksund* was due in Stavanger and could bring the loco across in about a week's time. The price would be £8,500 and was I more agreeable? I was not. "Then what will you pay?" came the next question. Quick thinking was called for. "Not more than £5,000," I replied, doubting if this would be accepted but with no idea of what his bottom figure would be. "OK – we bring it," came his swift answer.

When No 5856 (the NSB number) arrived at Felixstowe, it was the ship's only cargo. I then learned that but for the loco it would have come over empty for, having discharged at Stavanger, it was due to come to Felixstowe to pick up another cargo. But this was by the way and, as the cranes at each end of the almost deckless ship lifted the loco onto the ramp rails leading to Sunter's transporter, we – Robert, Geoff and I – were fearful that such a machine would not be in running condition for another two years, for two years had already passed since the purchase was agreed upon. But, after a circuitous route to Bressingham, we found that its inward parts appeared to be sound and hopes rose as steam was raised with no leaks appearing. We also noticed that British-made new tyres had been fitted in 1952 and even if some retubing was to be expected, the boiler and firebox showed little sign of wastage from rust.

It had been built in Berlin by Borsig in 1944 and, despite Germany's plight at the time, nothing had been skimped in the building. As a Class, the 52s were more numerous than any other, anywhere. From a 1937 utility design it was known as the Krieglok and the 9–12,000 built were spread out all over Europe with a few minor variations. This one had a round bottom Vanderbilt type of tender and, although in a sense ugly in British eyes, it was not so in mine because it was so functional and yet simple.

Not so the 141 *Tom Paine* which was much more complicated, with several outside appendages and ranks of external piping. When steamed for testing, Geoff had some problems to solve with accessories which failed to function or were having to be tried out to discover what their function was. The cab was full of valves with no indication of their purpose. Some, low down,

German 2–10–0 'Krieglok' *built 1944, recovered from Norway.*

were obviously for the automatic stoker which drew down coal from the tender, crushed it and then steam ejected it on different parts of the grate as different valves were opened. Above, valves, gauges and levers on the face plate were marked with numbers or hieroglyphics, in French, or more often with no indication of their purpose. It needed someone with Geoff's knowledge to test them all and, once their use was known, he fixed labels to them. *Tom Paine* was steamed several times – seldom though without some defect or failure having to be put right. But the automatic stoker worked too well. It was so voracious for coal that its use had to be banned and our BR drivers anyway preferred to fire with a shovel.

In between times two other steam engines on wheels had come unobtrusively into the collection. One of these was an 0–4–0 crane engine from the Doxford Company at Sunderland. It had a

Key helpers at Bressingham pose on the French 1–4–1 of 156 tons 'Tom Paine' *built in the USA.*

semi-vertical boiler with a short but fairly massive crane of several tons' capacity which, when out of use, rested upon the chimney ahead. It was specially designed and built by Robert Stephenson and Hawthorne in 1942 for ship repair work or possibly ship building, since it was capable of passing over ships' plates. It was bought by Jim Price in the name of his second son and, although not sufficiently versatile for us to use often, it made a very interesting exhibit once Don had given it his full treatment in royal blue paint. Another was simply a dockside crane which had become redundant at Felixstowe port. With its tall galvanised cab over the vertical boiler it was no beauty but, having a 20 feet jib able to lift and sway five tons, it was occasionally useful until the boiler became more than merely suspect. It remains, to my shame, the only steamer never to be restored to its original appearance.

Don Hubbard works on restoration.

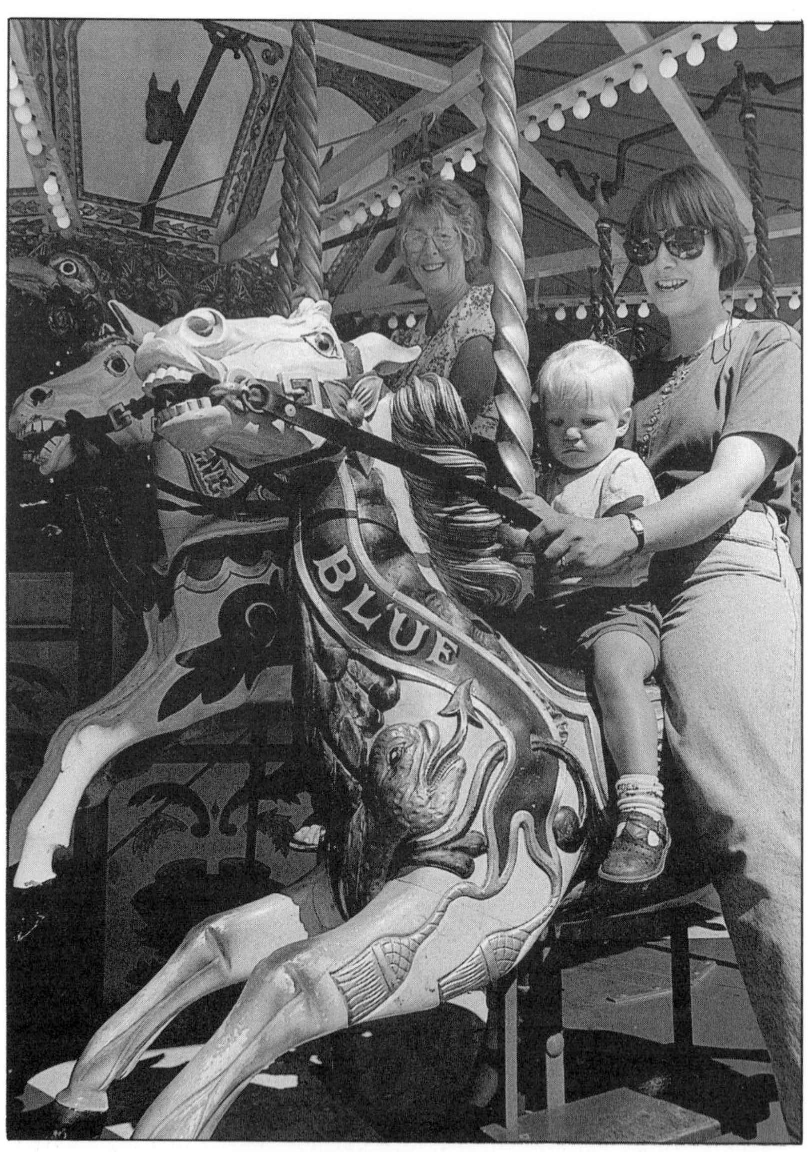

Visitors enjoying themselves on the 'Gallopers'.

CHAPTER TWELVE

BIRTH PANGS FOR THE IMMORTAL

Over the 15 years – 1961 to 1976 – the addition of the two foreigners had brought the total number of steam engines on wheels to 40, about half road and half rail users. But once I began to look beyond my personally owned traction engines as scope for a comprehensive museum opened up, it had to include engines and steam powered equipment for which wheels were not required. The most important of those acquired was the set of gallopers – steam horses or roundabouts. An integrally genuine part of a set was already on show to visitors in steam on its little trailer. It was the Tidman Centre engine and a handicapped pensioner, Bert Swann, was just the man to look after it. On more than one occasion he'd made wistful hints that we only needed the set of gallopers for it to drive, especially when the Steam Gala event came round with Screeton Brothers' splendid set on hire for the event. As with other old-time equipment, especially if steam driven, prices were soaring and, as antique works of art, so ornate, with a genuine organ for the music, the possibility of being able to buy one seemed remote at that time – when both Adrian and Robert were about to marry and needing a house – in addition to a nursery expansion programme afoot.

Then came two unexpected windfalls. At first I'd bluntly refused to consider selling the faulty, unpopular Marshall traction engine but when the prospective buyer offered what was then a very good price, and when Jack Clements advised me to let it go, it was followed by the addition of several more hundreds from an old endowment policy maturing. Premiums having been paid by banker's order, I'd almost forgotten it. The two sums together, I hoped, might go a fair way to buying a set of gallopers, not merely to satisfy Bert Swann or myself, but to give Flora a pleasurable involvement, knowing her affection for such old time rides and for mechanical organs. For a few weeks I kept the

The Gallopers

The gallopers' engine fully restored; Roger Garnham at the controls.

notion to myself and scanned the *World's Fair* advertisements week by week. And then, in the autumn issue of 1967 there it was – a set with no engine, but with an organ at a price well below what I had expected.

"Would it appeal to you", I asked Flora, "to have a set of gallopers of your own?"

Her eyes lit up quizzically. "You know very well there's nothing I'd like more – but what's the idea? You can't afford to buy a set so you must be just teasing."

I assured her I was not and then told her what was in my mind. It had occurred often enough that over the years my avidity for collecting engines had been to some extent at her expense. There had been times when I'd put engines first, either through skimping improvements inside the home or through being too preoccupied with restoration work to take a break with her away from home. Now, with money matters improving, there might be a good chance of expressing appreciation in a tangible way by making her a present which could be in keeping with the steam collection as a whole. If I got a set of old-time roundabouts, powered by the Tidman Centre engine, it would be complete. And Bert Swann too would have his dearest wish fulfilled.

Roger was all in favour of such an acquisition. Though so dedicated to steam, he had in earlier years had leanings towards showground equipment, being especially thrilled by fair organs and the less modern rides such as gallopers. He had also considerable musical gifts of his own and, apart from often playing an electronic organ at dances, was a regular church organist in his native parish of Garboldisham. It was in fact his copy of *World's Fair* which he had brought over in order to show me the advertisement for a set of gallopers.

Early one morning, Flora, Roger and I set off for Scotland, catching an Edinburgh train at Peterborough. But it was growing dark by the time we finally reached Ladybank, a small mining town in Fife, where the gallopers were still erected. It was one of those hurried deals – not only was time short but also I had more or less made up my mind in advance. The owners were fairground folk who had, I was soon able to discover, even more firmly made up their minds to sell, saying they believed some more modern type of ride would pay them better. They reckoned

The Gallopers "Bruder" organ.

Children enjoying a ride on the 'Gallopers'.

Santa gets ready to board one of his 'Specials' to greet the many young visitors who come to Bressingham every year.

too that modern canned music was more popular than music from an organ and, because of this, theirs was seldom used. All it needed, they said, was tuning; knowing no better, we believed them. When it was played for our benefit some almost unrecognisable tunes emerged until we asked them to switch off the blaring, jarring noises it made. But, because they were willing to come down well below the advertised price and deliver the set to Bressingham and because they seemed pretty genuine people, we clinched the deal within an hour, over a high tea they provided for us.

It was dawn again when we left the night mail train at Peterborough after a sleepless night because the only passenger coach was so full. For a week we could scarcely believe the reality of what we'd done. But there was no doubt about it when two large ancient lorries arrived, each with its trailer. One lorry, with generator underslung, was left behind after the other had disgorged its 36 horses, ostriches and cockerels, sadly tarnished and chipped but still gaudy. Left in the yard under its tarpaulin stood the centre truck, bringing back, in a different context, memories of a sight which had struck terror in my early childhood. It still looked like a gun carriage, with the centre pole folded down just like the barrel of a cannon, grimly menacing.

Flora was quick to find out more about its history. The makers were Savages of King's Lynn, who were still functioning as an engineering firm. She learned that the horses and birds had been hand carved, probably before it was made into a steam-driven set in the 1890s. The organ's history was more difficult to trace, but most likely it was made in Germany about the same period, judging by the dress of the carved little figures poised in front as conductor and shepherdesses to tinkle little bells. Thrilled to bits, Flora could scarcely wait to make a start on the long process of restoration, beginning with the horses. "It will take me years", she said, "but it's got to be right, and I want to do all the repainting myself."

It was the variety, it seemed, that attracted visitors to Bressingham in increasing numbers. The whole thing was snowballing and not the least important new feature for 1968 was Flora's gallopers. She had spent all available time for months past in repainting the horses, ostriches and cockerels which now glinted so splendidly in the light. Most of them were horses, some with intricately carved manes and, with Adrian's wife Rosemary to help, one by one they had had their gay patterns lovingly traced and coloured with flamboyant paint and were stored up in a spare bedroom until all 30 were ready. I was doing a series of Gardening Spots in Anglia's 'At Home' programme during that time. The TV unit came one day for this but, as soon as they saw Flora and Rosemary at work, the producer changed his mind and my gardening demonstration had to take second place.

We built up the gallopers just south of the office, where for years a little patch of ground had been used for heeling in plants. Now it was sown to grass and the centre truck with its grimly cannon-like folded chimney was placed in position. Around this, until its chassis was completely hidden, the ancient set was built up, with the organ facing one way and the Tidman Centre engine the other. Bert Swann came to inspect and boards were laid to form gently sloping gang planks so that he could shuffle up on those legs of his that would not bend. The perch beside his engine was less handy now than before but, because the Tidman was now to serve the purpose for which it was made, he was highly delighted. On the rounding board, instead of the former high-falutin' showman's advertisement was the legend – 'The Bressingham Steam Roundabouts, Built by Norfolk Craftsmen when Victoria was Queen'. And when it began to revolve, with mirrors flashing, with the bright paintwork glinting under the lights and the organ playing, it was very attractive. Even so, it was annoying when now and then someone referred to it as a 'hurdy-gurdy' or asked if the next thing would be a coconut-shy or hoop-la. To us, as to most people, it was an antique of a very nostalgic and colourful type, not out of place because of its steam element. It would give innocent pleasure to lots of people and, if what they paid for rides would enable Flora over the years to restore it fully, then she too would be content.

Too readily perhaps I had seen Flora's ownership of the gallopers as a means of augmenting her income – apart from the added attraction it would be for the visitors. What I did not realise was the extent to which she would take it as a responsibility to ensure it was always in safe working condition, to protect it from such hazards as fire and gales, nor how thorough would be her standards of restoration and maintenance, aiming always for perfection. So it was that it took several years before takings for rides showed any appreciable rewards for her labours and costs where repair work had to be done by others. Examples of the latter were a complete new floor to replace the ancient, gaping wooden structure; a new centre pole on which the set hung – and which was also a chimney for the engine which had worn dangerously thin and was made of heavy steel tube which was very expensive; the cranks which made the horses gallop in uncomfortable jerks had to be renewed and there were almost annual repairs needed for the organ as well as card music to renew and enhance with additional tunes; tilts and side curtains did not last many years, some having been torn off by gales.

Over these anxious years, however, its popularity with visitors never slackened and when at last the set reached the standard Flora had set, then came some reward. Pleasure as well as ongoing commitment was shared by her two equally devoted helpers, Dennis Leeper and Jack Barber, who took over when Bert Swann died. Its site between the nursery offices, later converted to visitors' tea-rooms and the main museum building is thereabouts ideal. Unlike most remaining old-time sets which have to be dismantled frequently for moving from place to place, it can stay put from April until the end of September. Over winter it is in store under cover but there was an occasion when a store shed caught fire and nine of the wooden horses were destroyed and replacements proved hard to find.

The concept of a comprehensive live steam museum could not exclude stationary industrial engines. Of those still to be found, many were massive and one needed to be realistic. As a means of power they were historically a century ahead of road and rail using engines – and this was also true of marine engines which offered the least prospect of fitting in with my live museum ambitions. The stationary type which appealed to me was a beam engine, with memories of the one for draining Over Fen, which fascinated me as a boy. With its oscillating beam it was an archetype for there was no other in the era of Newcomen and Watt during the 18th century and beam engines for industry were in use till far into the 20th. The first stationary engine to come to Bressingham was believed to be over 100 years old but it was neither the beam type nor very large. It came from a local factory with no maker's name and was simply a vertical cylinder with piston and flywheel, weighing very little and taking up very little space. Not so the next one, which became something of an

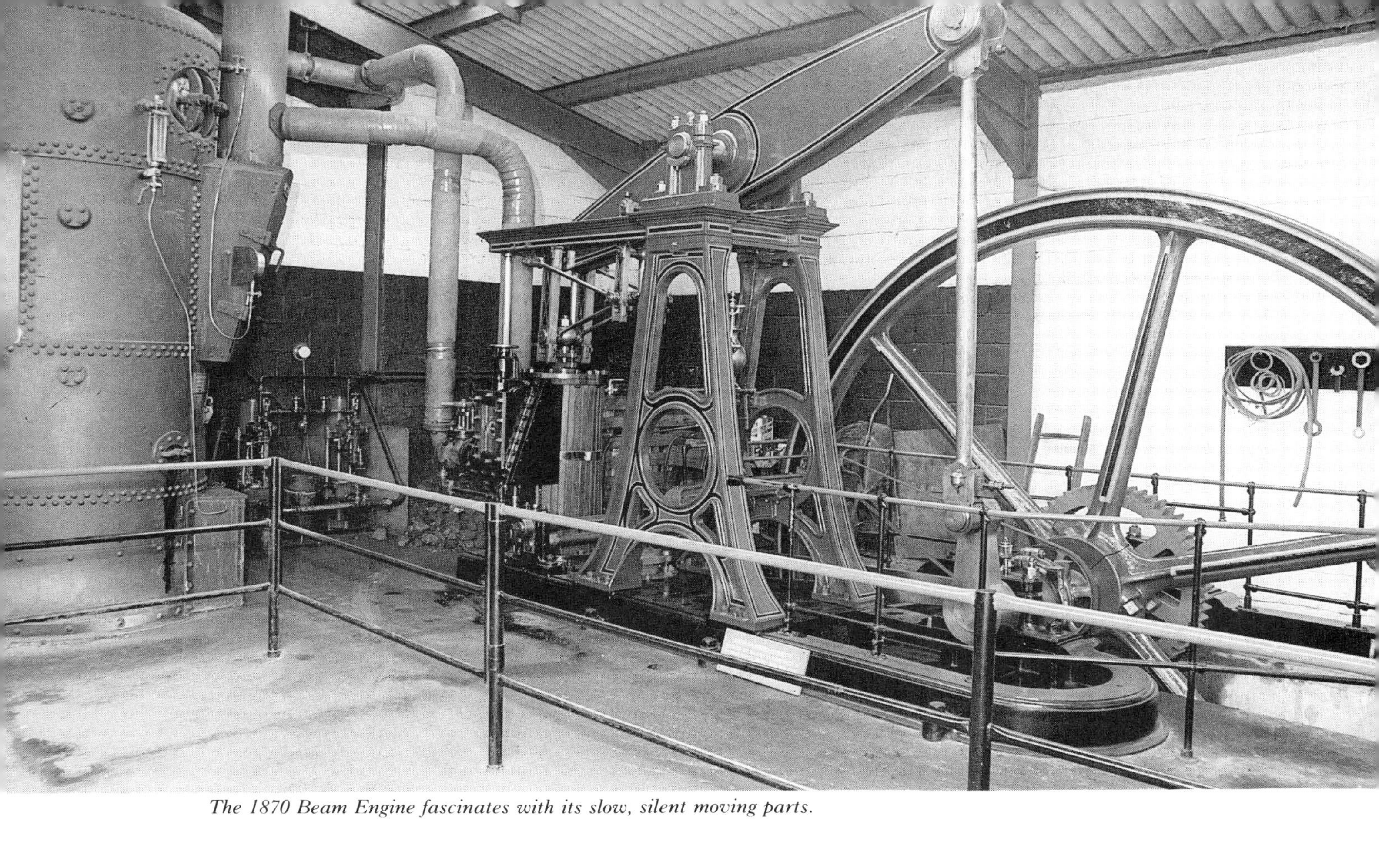

The 1870 Beam Engine fascinates with its slow, silent moving parts.

The Manager of Chivers Jam Factory restarts Sir William Arrol *after restoration.*

Full view of Arrol Horizontal Pumping Engine of 1905.

embarrassment as it lay in pieces for several years outside the shed because we had neither the space nor time to put it together again.

This horizontal type, built by Guest and Craven about 1880, was presented by Wards Sawmill of Boxmoor, Hertfordshire, leaving us only the cost of transport to bear. A long crankshaft turned a 12 feet diameter flywheel weighing eight tons, also activated a suction pump whilst the flywheel, duly belted, drove the mill machinery. Two other horizontal engines were representatives of the smaller stationaries by Marshalls of Gainsborough, who also built traction engines. One was twice the size of the other and both possessed a single cylinder as was common for relatively slow running. The required speed of the machinery they powered was regulated by the size of pulleys turned by belts from the engine flywheel. Over the years several other small engines and steam pumps came our way. These included a Gwynne vertical reciprocating pumping engine of 1905 from Framlingham College, and a Merryweather fire engine pump which had probably been taken from a horse-drawn fire brigade outfit and adapted as a standby for the brush factory at Diss. A bilge pump, Weir boiler pump and an engine of the type used for a steam shovel were also put aside for later assembly. These accumulations did not go on proper display until the mid-1970s. Until then all our efforts had been directed on to railway locos but, when the offer came of a very heavy steam generator from St Andrew's Hospital in Norwich, an immediate permanent site was called for. This Bellis & Morcom incorporated quite late developments of steam power with compounding cylinders able to attain a drive shaft speed of 600 rpm on to the 230 volt DC dynamo – all in one unit standing six feet high. The time had come then to oust the traction engines ranged against the west wall of the big shed. Bedded in or on concrete blocks, the stationary engines made quite an impressive range as, having installed the largest exhibits, the smaller ones came out of hiding to take up spaces between them. The job was finished off by making up a mock faceplate of a Lancashire type boiler, complete with fire doors and fittings. Fixed to the wall with a brick surround it was realistic enough to prompt a few visitors to go outside in search of the long boiler they expected to see on the other side.

Still no beam engine but by way of distraction from my search for one, there was now the need for another building in which to house the traction engines as well as one or two other stationaries still not installed. To the east of the gallopers and nursery offices now converted into a tea-room with a south facing verandah was what had been the nursery packing shed. I'd built it in 1948 and, though its coverage had more than doubled by 1968, it then became redundant when a huge 'production unit' and packing shed, along with new offices, were built as a result of Robert's and Adrian's expansionist drive. My own ambitions for the museum had reached a kind of peak so far as representative collection of engines was concerned. But it was becoming increasingly obvious that more cover would be needed for the traction engines and the steady accumulation of small items from railway lamps to number plates, name boards and models, many of which had been presented to us by well-wishers.

The kind of building we needed would be large and costly, because adequate toilets and a shop area were becoming a vital necessity. My makeshifting was becoming intolerable. Having seen the need for another large building looming up, I also saw it as the final phase of development. The collecting phase had to end at the point or time when it became evident that we had acquired enough exhibits, live or static, to care for. But if caring spelt housing as a prime necessity, as it did, then it needed to be carefully planned. And because funds and seasonal receipts would not stand the cost of an adequate building, a bank loan appeared to be inevitable. Partly to avoid this for as long as possible, Robert and I designed one of 7,000 square feet, to which an even larger section would be added a year or two later. It did not take long to erect and, apart from the concrete floor, it was all metal. In went the traction engines and two threshing drums, plus the two steam fire engines. One of these was a hand-hauled portable – the type used for emergencies during World War I. The other was a marvellous example of splendour with which the Victorians embellished a utility. It had been installed beneath Sir J J Colman's mansion near Norwich in 1895. Shand Mansion was a leading make with an upright flash boiler and double acting pumps which were, it was said, capable of dousing a fire with water within five minutes from cold. What caught the gaze, however, was its display of polished brass and copper sheeting, wherever it could be placed with effect, though it must be allowed that they were also the best materials for the job.

This splendid exhibit – never to be other than static – had come to us through the good offices of Jack Sutton about to retire as Inspecting Engineer for the Regional Hospitals' Authority – the Colman mansion had become a geriatric home. Jack had put other exhibits and equipment our way, as well as being a driver on our Waveney Valley Railway. There were, it seemed, no beam engines needing a home to be found anywhere in East Anglia and when one was at last located, of a size we could house, it came from a Surrey hospital, assisted by a man who became not only a friend indeed to the museum, and a trustee, but a dear family friend as well.

I first met Sir David Follett as Director of the Science Museum in London. That was when the British Railways Historical Relics were handed over to the Department of Education and Science to make Sir David responsible for them. Having four from the now National Collection on loan at Bressingham, John Scholes came to inspect. John, incidentally, had decided to learn the art of engine driving at Bressingham in hopes of future application when the Clapham Collection moved elsewhere. Sir David also became interested and obviously enjoyed coming, with engines, garden and Flora's hospitality all a draw. He retired in 1973 and the next year he and I took a steam railway based holiday together in India – an unforgettable experience for us both. At Bressingham his way of showing his interest appealed to our workshop staff – as it did for the garden helpers – and his counsel on such matters as museum display was invaluable.

When the time came, after a good season in 1979, to go ahead with the final phase, the old packing sheds were demolished and the carefully planned building began, though not without serious snags initially. To level up with the recently erected section, the north end of the floor needed prior excavation to four feet below land level. But when a spring of water with running sand was revealed at one corner the planners insisted on so much more reinforcement of the foundations that it cost an extra £2,000 in steel rods in addition to the hefty bank loan. There were other minor snags as well, all adding up to a total cost of £120,000. But here at last were ample and very smart toilets, and Mary Fox could happily move out of the ex-BR brakevan which had served as gift and souvenir shop for years. And above the toilets and shop was a gallery for the welter of small exhibits awaiting display, in a dozen show cases on stout tables provided for us by Sir David Follett. We labelled the new building 'Exhibition Hall' to distinguish it from the locomotive museum across the way. To offset its plain exterior I built in panels of colourful stones and Norfolk flints, having practised a technique I discovered when needing retaining walls in the garden. Inside there was ample room both for a wide variety of static exhibits and for visitors to inspect them even when heavy showers drove them in to take cover. All told, we now had nearly an acre under cover and there was room too for a Royal Coach, which came on offer in 1982. This splendid vehicle of 45 tons weight on which no expense had been spared, was built in 1908 for HM King Edward VII and Queen Alexandra. As a day coach, it had lounges and writing rooms, toilets and bath and, though the public was not allowed inside, a platform was made from which to peep into the luxurious lighted compartments. By way of contract, visitors stared at models of various model engines in cases, many on loan from people who wished to share their possessions with others. A Norfolk farmer, Mr Lewin, had spent years in building a threshing set with engine which was so perfect in every detail that it would thresh corn, scaled down though it was, and beside it stood a miniature ploughing engine faithful in every detail.

We missed Sir David sorely when he died in 1982. He had been a good friend in so many ways. In their way, so had several others who had helped both as regulars and volunteers. Geoff Sands had put us right when we were most likely to have erred without his knowledge and experience. But having semi-retired because of heart trouble and moved away, he succumbed to an attack just before reaching his fiftieth year. Ben Francis and Arthur Prentice, buddies and at loggerheads with one another in turn, both died within months of each other. Jack Clements continued on doggedly until well into his eighties, by which time Roger brought him in by car, to work as best he could. Now, facing the Gallopers are several seats for visitors and each one records that it was placed there in memory of those helpers who have passed on. But on the balustrade of the upper floor of the Exhibition Hall is a much larger, longer notice. It reads: 'The Sir David Follett Gallery'.

Knowing of my long-standing wish to add a beam engine to the collection, Sir David had unobtrusively set about finding one. He finally located one about to be made redundant at the Banstead Hospital in Surrey. He concluded all the somewhat complicated negotiations with the Kensington, Chelsea and Westminster Hospital Authority so that it became a presentation to the museum. It was not a large one as beam engines go, with a 14 feet diameter flywheel and a 10 feet beam, but large enough to require an extension to be built on the front end of the museum. It also took Roger and Philip several days to dismantle it and, after it was delivered, to put it together again, with a deep trench in which the flywheel dipped as it revolved. Jack Sutton located an upright boiler from a Felixstowe hospital and, although he remained with us to see the engine working, Sir David did not. The boiler was only large enough to activate the 1870 Easton and Anderson beam engine and the most recent acquisition from Chivers jam factory at Histon. This was built by Sir William Arrol & Co Ltd of Glasgow and installed to operate a lift to upper floors of the factory. My intention to have others of these engines in slow motion on open days has still to be fulfilled. The beam engine alone brings people in to stand and stare at the slow, silent turning and thrusting of its moving parts.

Sir David had taken a special interest in the workshop – a vital adjunct which evolved more or less alongside the steadily increasing need to cope with restoration and repair work. The contract in workshop facilities between the early 1960s and the late 1970s was not so much one of ancient and modern as far as methods were concerned, but in scope and size. In moving over completely from the farm buildings, the east bay of the big locomotive shed was emptied of narrow gauge locos in the knowledge that more machine tools and other equipment would be needed when and as that need arose, consistent with what we could afford. For the evicted narrow gauge locomotives a lean-to shed outside was erected, just wide enough and long enough to hold the five 60 centimetre locos we then possessed. It was a squeeze until later the Swarzkopff was sold as being superfluous. With a workshop space of 100 feet by 24 feet, one end was converted into a lock-up stores for small spares from gauges to rivets, with a mess room above for the staff.

By degrees the spacious workshop became thereabouts full, with both 60 centimetre and 15 inch tracks for locomotive repairs, with work or inspection pits having removable covers. A gantry, sheet metal rollers, lathes, drills – including a large radial type – welders, grinders and virtually everything we were likely to need as well as work benches. Philip Gray quickly became an expert with a rare ability to overcome mechanical jobs by clever scheming which offered no easy way out. Roger, always patient and adaptable, was an unfailing standby but when someone had to take the lead as foreman he preferred to let Philip do so. A new dimension to their working capability came when, in addition to the carpenter's shop, a forge was built on to the rear of the big shed. This strip, shaded by chestnut trees, had been the Woodland Line Station and now, with rails laid in a concrete floor, boilers for the smaller locomotives could be made with George Garrard as the top expert. This was a task requiring knowledge, skill and often sheer muscle power. It took a long time to complete the first one for *Bronwllyd* but it was good to hear the boiler inspector say that it would outlast the lives of most of those who built it.

Stanley Clark, a retired master carpenter working next door to the forge, would not or could not skimp a job. I asked him to mend a straw elevator to go with the threshing set. So far as I could see it needed only a few timbers replaced but once it came under Stanley's charge I lost control over what repairs he should or should not make. He quietly went to work on it in his own way till the end result was virtually a new implement, employing such perfect workmanship with a young learner to help, that at no stage had I the heart to tell him it was costing too much in time and materials. It was much the same with George Garrard who, though not on the staff, spent most of his time in the workshop, year in and year out. Any impatience on my part as to the progress of some job he was engaged upon – such as a query about how much longer it would take to finish in anticipation of the next priority, would never elicit a straight answer. All I would get would be silence until he was fitting the next welding rod. "Well, there you are." This, in course of time and experience of George's attitude, had to be interpreted as simply, "I'll be finished when I'm satisfied that it's properly done and I can't say when that will be, so you'd best leave me to do it in my own way."

It took me a long time to separate Philip Gray from the steam-struck schoolboy that he once was to the skilled man he became. The top position in the workshop was filled by Eddie Wilkinson when Geoff Sands had to give up. He had been with the Festiniog Railway and no doubt Philip learned something from him too, quietly storing it away. Eddie made some useful improvements to the workshop but left after about two years to forsake steam for more money. It was then that, with Roger's reluctance to be in the position of staff control, the foreman's job was offered to Philip. Though half Roger's age, he soon proved both his skill and resourcefulness. He was fully competent to drive any of the engines, road or rail, large or small, as well as the old ex-WD Scammel tank transporter tractor with its winch for heavy hauls. He can use any of the machine tools and tackle any mechanical repairs with nonchalant expertise, and can scheme ways of saving time and labour, short of skimping, when thoroughness is the best policy. For someone with none of these skills, to be their boss calls for diplomacy and consideration on my part, based on thankfulness for their loyalty.

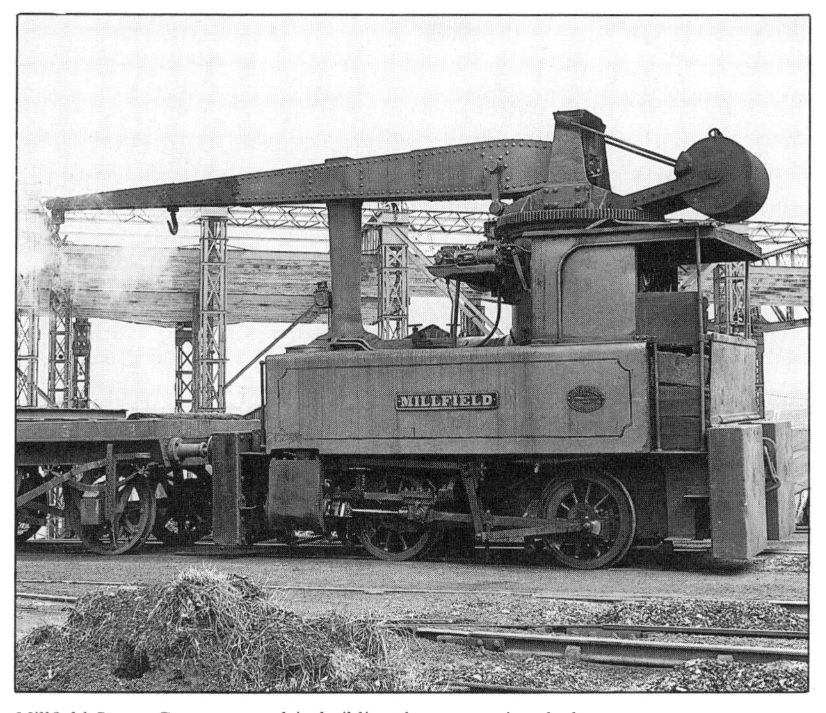

Millfield Steam Crane *engaged in building the new engine shed.*

6100 Royal Scot – *Dawn arrival after three day journey from Skegness.*

Steam up! – A plethora of engines outside the Museum.

The Railway Museum in the course of construction.

CHAPTER THIRTEEN

CHARITY BEGINS AT HOME

In certain circumstances the cussed part of my nature was apt to emerge when a course I had taken was challenged. When the garden was first opened to the public in 1957 the object was – apart from some pleasure in showing it to others – to be of some benefit to what I saw as good causes such as the NSPCC, medical research and Dr Barnardos. By 1967, when the sums so raised were twentyfold or more, I was still inclined to ignore such remarks as 'charity begins at home'. Over those 10 years some £33,000 gate money had been donated to a dozen or so charities including those whose local representatives or supporters manned the gate and parking. This was an easy, reciprocal arrangement and there was never a lack of volunteers. By 1965 railway rides were bringing in additional income and, because this ranked for Income Tax, our then accountant advised my firm to take over running costs by becoming owners of the rolling stock and thus keep on the right side of the Inland Revenue. So it was that the new locomotive shed also became a landlord's charge, but the influx of the standard gauge locomotives in 1968 put a very different complexion on the steam venture.

The scope and prospects of a live steam museum had in 1968 quite suddenly opened out. It could no longer be merely a hobby or whim if it were to expand – for which the new shed was a provision. Nor could there be a continuation of the ideal of giving gate money to charities when a large engine cost well into four figures for transport, to say nothing of subsequent costs of restoration. Wishing as I did to avoid any snare or accusation of being out for personal profit, the obvious answer would be to turn the steam museum as a whole into a charity on its own. Properly registered and run, I could then hand over my personally owned traction engines and, freed of tax liability, could go full steam ahead with development. But not so, said the Charity Commissioners. As the law stood I would have to step aside, for an owner could not play a part in fostering a venture based on his own property and subsidised by him. It must be handed over to an approved Board of Trustees which would have sole control and ownership. This was how the law stood then and it was so depressing and frustrating as to leave no way out – or way in as instigator and manager.

The immediate problem was in paying transport costs of the large locomotives. There was no telling, our accountant told us, how Revenue would view such expenditure, partly because it was by way of capital outlay. In his opinion it was safe from tax if paid as donations, for standard gauge engines must rank as capital and tax-chargeable expenses. Scouting about for safety, the newly established Transport Trust appeared to be a means to an end. Contact was made and its Council expressed willingness to cooperate. If we supplied them funds from the separate bank account into which gate receipts had always been paid, then the Trust would pay the bills for transporting the locomotives to Bressingham. As an alleviation and a means of avoiding tax liability on monies which were certainly not mine, this arrangement was good enough to let me forge ahead. But not without misgivings coupled with a sense of grievance because I could not openly and legitimately form a Charitable Trust which had no other objective than to preserve and bring back to life objects of widespread nostalgic and historical interest and value, excepting of course the personal joy and satisfaction of having them on my doorstep to share with others.

There still remained, however, the underlying anxiety of how to ensure that the museum and its exhibits, including those I personally owned, continued beyond my lifetime. I could will the latter to avoid duty so long as I survived for seven years thereafter. But it was not the answer, because they could scarcely be entailed to avoid dispersal, made more fraught because they were now worth so much more than when I bought them. Feeling driven up into a corner, I saw no way out other than to link up with the Transport Trust under a kind of legal umbrella. This appealed to its trustees far more than to me, for in law they would own or be custodians of all but the narrow gauge, then still owned by Bloom's Nurseries Ltd. Negotiations began early in 1970 involving visits to London for consultation and advice from counsel as well as visits by the Trust's officials to Bressingham.

The main sticking point was control of finance. To keep within the law, the Transport Trust would have to take all net gate receipts. And any undertaking on their part to devote all of them to the maintenance as well as expansion and development at Bressingham would demand watertight guarantees. Not to worry, the Secretary assured me. The Trust's solicitor would see to it and every needful clause would be included in the agreement. I gave in, having no alternative. The Trust was delighted, seeing Bressingham as its 'shop window' as it patted me on the back for being a public benefactor. In anticipation of the necessary handover documents being ready, 24 June 1972 was the date fixed well in advance for the handing over ceremony. The press was invited and engines were specially steamed when 24 June came. By then I'd swallowed but still not digested the niggling fears, not daring to tot up the total value I would be virtually giving away.

A vice-president of the Trust, General Lonsdale, had been appointed to receive the handover documents which the Secretary had brought back from the solicitor. And it was the General who took me aside to report that signing would have to come later because the wording was still incomplete, but would be within a week or two. A queer sense of relief for me, like a deferred sentence of execution, and on the surface it was a jolly day enjoyed by all. A month passed with no more developments and so far as I was concerned, the longer the final act was postponed, the better.

Those documents were never signed. Robert Manning, my solicitor, who had been acting on my behalf all along, came up with the news that the law which had prevented me from forming an independent Charitable Trust had just been changed and I was now free of restriction. The relief was almost overwhelming and I lost no time in telling the Transport Trust that the deal was off. With far more promptitude than that shown by its own solicitor, Robert applied for registration with the Charity Commissioners, but warned me that this was a slow moving body and could take up to a year. In the event, it took just long enough to cause more unexpected trouble – as a tail-piece to the marathon struggle. It began once the Inland Revenue got wind of the application for charitable status. My accountants – now a London firm – said that the Revenue would demand a declaration. This would be the only acceptable proof that both Flora and I had not used any receipts, going back to 1960, when the separate bank account had begun. They had consulted a specialist counsel who had pointed out that all those receipts should have been declared year by year, for in law they were taxable.

"You have a very good case for equity," the accountant said, "and so long as you've not fiddled any of the money, you should be exempt. All you and your wife have to do is to search back and list all private payments and receipts and we will audit them for presentation to the Tax Inspector. It may take time, but it'll be worth it – and of course the Revenue will demand it to be done."

The research took many, many tedious hours before our respective records, including household purchases, could be sent off to be prepared for the Tax Inspector. It was mitigated in a peculiarly annoying way, by the knowledge that no fiddling had ever taken place, if only from the very cussedness referred to in the first sentence of this chapter. But it took the accountants a year to prepare, which brought a bill for over £2,000 to which counsel's and other fees were added. So began a ding-dong battle between them and the Tax Inspector, continuing for 19 years after the first approach and 9 years after the museum became registered as a charity in its own right in August 1973. Over that period there were more consultations involving two other counsels and total bills in excess of £6,000 for fees. During most of that time the accountants stuck out for equity, though it became clear that strictly in line with the law, those gate receipts should have paid tax before being distributed to charities. But neither the London firm nor the local firm of accountants had given any previous warning that this was so and when finally the accountants caved in by accepting a deal with the Inspector for a reduced liability of £12,500, with it came a string of recommendations that I too should accept and pay up lest the Inspector demand his full pound of flesh. I saw red and told him I'd fight it out on my own. That was the measure of my sense of injustice. The accountants may have decided they'd had enough in spite of them telling me so often that the time was on my side. But I suspected they had made a blunder or two or some misjudgement, and for all the equity I felt was on my side the Inspectors were suavely telling me at an interview that they had made many concessions already. I firmly believed that my operation had all along been as if it were a registered charity and even the half pound of flesh they were demanding would be cruel and unjust. They then said I had right of appeal to the Commissioners of Inland Revenue. There were two separate bodies, one consisting of lawyers and the other of laymen. Naturally choosing the latter, the Inspectors did not warn me that in the circumstances I should have gone to the former since my appeal was not against the actual computation but a protest against the application of the letter of the law – based on equity. The hearing took place in Norwich in April 1983 and I read out a 17 page plea. Having done so, the Inspector then asked if I disagreed with the computation of their assessment, to which I could but answer "no". My protest was against the liability for tax in the circumstances. They then called for the appeal to be dismissed because those General Commissioners who had listened and spoken much sympathy for my plight so far, were not in law competent to pass judgement. Only then did I realise I should have gone to the Special Commissioners with my appeal.

It was from museum funds that the £12,500 had to be paid for I'd already paid over £6,000 in fees. I simply had not the means to pay it myself. It was then ruled out of time to continue the fight to the last ditch with the Special Commissioners. I could but cut back on the list of engines in need of restoration. One of them was the *Royal Scot*, which had to be taken out of service because of faulty tubes and perhaps firebox repairs being required. In the three of four years it had been giving footplate rides it had been as popular as *Oliver Cromwell*, whilst the latter was under repair, and in 1978 it was this famous LMS locomotive which figures in a very different tussle with some official upholders of bureaucracy which they did not win.

It began on a fine afternoon in mid-August 1978. A good crowd boosted by holiday-makers was as usual enjoying this outing where gardens and steam, so diverse, were so uniquely complementary. From my elevated position on the footplate of

Gwynedd it was interesting to study faces as people passed or paused. But neither I nor any of us in charge one way or another would have suspected that one of the thousands present was a furtive Government Inspector out to find fault if he could. That he did without reference to anyone present was evident from a telephone call from the Railway Inspectorate next morning, announcing that a ban was being placed on footplate riding. This was followed up by the official order on the grounds of imminent danger to the public, on pain of a £400 penalty. In protest I telephoned back next day to say that over the years about 25,000 people had enjoyed the thrill without a single mishap or hurt to anyone. The reply was that their opinion stood and there was imminent danger especially as the visiting inspector had calculated speeds of up to 30 mph being reached. I could appeal if I wished. It was my legal right, but it would be a waste of time to do so. Their injunctions were virtually indisputable.

In consultation with Robert Manning our trustee solicitor, and David Ward as a BR official familiar with the Inspectorate's scope and reputation, we decided to appeal to the appropriate Industrial Tribunal. But till then the ban was in force and there stood *Royal Scot* for the rest of the season, carrying a notice I'd made giving the reason why visitors were not allowed to ride. Meanwhile, counsel and a junior were briefed and a date in November was fixed for the three-man Tribunal to hear the appeal in the Magistrate's Courtroom of Diss Corn Hall. Publicity was not lacking and the *Eastern Daily Press* included the case in its editorial, as well as readers' letters in our favour. There were the two involved officials of the Railway Inspectorate (a Government appointed body independent of BR) and their solicitor present, whilst the public gallery was well filled with press and other interested people, including, of course, some of our own BR drivers and one or two steam loco experts to be called as witnesses if need be. The Inspector's case rested, they said, on long experience. Accidents liable to cause injury to those on the footplate of a locomotive in steam had happened before and could happen again. Water gauge glasses were known to shatter and emit scalding steam – as could many other pipes and joints on the face plate. A blow-back through the firebox door could also occur and even if any of these hazards caused no injury they could create panic on a crowded footplate with risk of people being seriously injured by falling headlong out of the door on to the track several feet below. The Inspectorate's infallible rule was that only one person as a special favour was allowed on the footplate, and then only if under the supervision of a competent railway official, to ensure safety and prevent distraction to the driver and fireman. When asked by counsel how the furtive inspector had calculated that *Royal Scot* was being driven at speeds up to 30 mph, he proudly stated that it was by means of checking driving wheel revolutions with the second hands of his watch.

This was challenged and refuted as was the rule of only one footplate passenger. Our side pointed out that whilst it would be a wise safety rule on an engine pulling a passenger train, the matter of risks to footplate riders at Bressingham devolved on whether or not they were in imminent danger. When asked to define the word 'imminent', the furtive inspector failed to do so, but declared that he knew more about locomotives than anyone else present. Counsel took advantage of this by calling an expert witness who made nonsense of his claim, saying that if the footplate was so dangerous why was anyone allowed either up there or to stand beside an engine driver where there were other pipes and fittings under steam pressure. More questions were put by counsel which brought more confusion to the Inspector and not even his supporting solicitor could help him out.

The hearing lasted two days and, although our hopes of winning had steadily risen, the Tribunal Chairman gave no hint of this. He was very alert, very meticulous, but very fair, but in closing the proceedings said that no verdict would be given until after he and his two colleagues had inspected *Royal Scot*'s footplate. A week or two later they came, with Geoff Sands and a BR driver, to explain how things worked and how hazards were minimised, and also what the procedure would be should something go wrong. The next request was to call up our helpers on to the footplate. They stood just as if there were 10 visitors footplate riding, leaving space for driver and foreman to be free, as was our rule, to cope with any emergency. When fully satisfied with this phase, we were told that the Tribunal would make a public announcement in due course. It was worth waiting for and certainly had been worth fighting for. We had won, it seemed, a famous victory. The Inspectorate's rulings had apparently never before been challenged, much less dismissed, with an order to pay costs which included our counsel's hefty fees.

This case is not described in order to imping the Railway Inspectorate as a body, but just to show how minor officials can cause trouble for themselves and to others through excessive zeal. In later dealings with higher ranking officials of the Inspectorate I became much more aware of its true purpose – of safeguarding public safety with a minimum of interference with railway operators who themselves are safety conscious.

Since then the number of footplate passengers has risen to between 90–100,000, still with no damage or hurt to anyone. As the Tribunal members were told, any pipe or fitting on the faceplate is regularly tested and gauge glasses renewed. Safe limits on speed and on the number of riders are strictly observed by all drivers. But if the charge of imminent danger was preposterous, steam under pressures of up to 240 psi has to be constantly respected. There are hazards, but care and constant vigilance reduce risks to the irreducible minimum. On a statistical basis, the Bressingham record cannot be compared with any other steam centre or railway, because it remains the only place where it is practised. Compared with some other forms of entertainment, however, where machines are the draw, it is less dangerous to the public than such as motor racing and some fairground amusements.

Sadly, *Royal Scot* has not been steamed since 1978. It is 60 years old and needs to have a thorough examination of its boiler. Time was when we could be given insurance cover on the assurances of our trained, qualified helpers, largely because we had a clean record but in recent years regulations have become more stringent. Cases of negligence resulting in damage and injury have occurred at a few steam centres, to scare insurance companies into demanding official inspections at stated intervals, and cover withheld until certificates of safety are issued. For some locomotives the boiler has to be lifted from the frame, all tubes removed before internal inspection can take place and, to examine the outer shell, the casing and lagging has to come off. If, as often is the case, the lagging all round is of asbestos, then the whole operation becomes very expensive indeed. The Health and Safety Authority has now become almost paranoic about asbestos. Only approved specialists are allowed to remove it by cocooning the whole thing under stipulated conditions. This process alone costs well into four figures for a boiler of moderate size. And my guess is that one by one, locos at steam centres and preserved railways will become permanently static because funds simply will not be available to keep them active. In addition to inspection costs, there will still be those boiler repairs to make, which official inspection reveals. When a boiler is condemned altogether the cost of a new one would be astronomical and impossible for most owners to reach.

For years our charge for adult footplate passengers has been 50p. It lasts only a few minutes on the 600 yard track up and down. It is a poor day indeed when it does not cover running costs, the greatest of which is coal. This vital commodity, by the way, cost £9 per ton 20 years ago when I first began to buy it for engines. Now, in 1991, it is at least £90 per ton. What passengers pay certainly does not cover the cost of major repairs and renewals, and yet I am always reluctant to step up charges, even to keep up with inflation. To be fully realistic in this respect would, I fear, be counter-productive. It is pleasing to hear visitors say they have had good value and I would find no joy in running the concern with them disgruntled at being charged prices realistic for us but expensive for them.

The locomotives comprising the National Collection in the care of the official railway museums are of course maintained at public expense. At present the public is admitted free of charge to see them in pristine condition – but lifeless. A few from the National Collection are on loan to approved railway centres where live steam is the thing, and if Bressingham is unique in giving footplate rides, the remaining few on loan are only occasionally used to haul special steam excursion trains. No contributions are made from the public purse to keep them active. In other words, the official view comes down heavily towards static display and not live steam, despite all the evidence that steam alive and active had infinitely greater public appeal. It seems doubtful if this official attitude will ever change, and it places a crippling disadvantage on private railway centres and museums which try to keep steam alive. This applies both to those of us who were amongst the early birds on the preservation scene, and to those who came later on the wave of nostalgia. The latter had to be content to purchase and restore what others had left, especially at Woodham's yard in South Wales, where most of the 300 or so BR locos have been saved from the torch by enthusiasts. They also bought up for preservation to run on abandoned BR branch lines any obsolete industrial locos however ugly and unglamorous. Steam nostalgia shows no sign of fading, and the very fact of it becoming more difficult to keep engines alive as time goes on may offset fears which some of us have had that satiation and diminishing returns would set in.

The surging, widening interest in steam would never have come about had it not been possible for some relics of the steam age to be brought back to active life. Of this there can be no doubt. For those of us old enough to remember steam as commonplace on the railways, roads and farms, it was accepted as if it would never be superseded. The fact is, that since the 1940s its disappearance from the everyday scene is a remarkable phenomenon not to be dismissed, to my way of thinking, as a peculiar but inexplicable outlet for mere nostalgia for days gone by. This may well be applicable for older folk, but can scarcely apply to the many under forty who are just as fascinated by steam alive, if not more so. This group includes many who have only seen preserved engines perhaps for the first time.

My own theory, as an explanation, is that steam alive affects something pretty deep in the human mind, be it subconscious or otherwise. It could well be an aspect of the Jungian collective unconscious, back to the remote past when homo sapiens became aware of the vital but dangerous elements of fire and water. Both were good servants but bad masters, powerful enough to be deified. To them it was probably a form of magic to discover that fire could produce hot water and so to boil food to become more palatable, and that water could quench fire. In course of time both elements were found to have other uses, all making for progress on the road to civilisation. But until the 17th century fire and water together made no further impact. Power sources were still those of wind, muscle and gravity impelled water. The first experiments led, by the early 18th century, to Newcomen's ponderous engines for mining, followed by James Watt's for both mining and industry. But these engines were not to be seen by the general public, few of whom would know of their existence apart from those who toiled in the dark satanic mills. And then

David Weston – the artist – discussing his work with Alan Bloom at an exhibition in the Railway Museum.

came Trevithick and Stephenson and others in the early 1800s with both road and railway locomotives and, for the first time, ordinary people were able to see what was to them the most magical invention of all time. For the first time in the long history of the human race these two vital elements of fire and water were seen acting upon one another to produce power and motion. There it was, smoke from the fire and steam from the water making wheels go round to pull loads which a score of horses could not budge. And for a few coppers, rides behind the iron horses could be taken at unheard of speeds. This, I believe, is the explanation of the fascination for steam and why it affects so many more now than in the hundred years or so when it was commonplace. Preservation of a relatively few engines – has rekindled this in a more numerous, more mobile and leisured population than was the case in the period of its first great impact, 150 or so years ago.

On this assumption, it would be safe to predict that steam in action will be as much an attraction 50 years – or 150 years – hence, as now. Rarity might have the effect of narrowing it down to places where funds have allowed new boilers to be made. For it is also safe to predict that any engine in steam now will have required a new boiler within 50 years. It is a somewhat sobering thing to reflect upon costs so far as the Bressingham road and rail using engines are concerned, if all were to be made safe to run with new boilers. Their total cost when new from the makers would be in the region of £150,000. To fit them all with new boilers would at present rates cost over 2 million.

Perhaps it's as well the future is obscured. To the wealthy few a million is not a vast sum. The Government can allocate such a sum or more for a purpose which may have no impact on the public weal, and every one of the many Tornado fighters which often pass over us with a terrifying roar, costs £15 million to build. The Government also hands out payments to those who cater for the tourist industry, be it for hotel extension or some purely commercial enterprise, designed to attract tourist or leisure seekers. Such grants are for capital outlay, but there were no grants available when buildings and installations were put up at Bressingham because East Anglia was not then designated as a tourist area. Buildings had to come first and over £200,000 was spent on proper housing of exhibits and visitor amenities before

Tourist Board grants became generally applicable.

And now, because we had put our priorities in the right order, fully intending to restore later to safe working condition all worthy and interesting engines enabling the general public to savour all the power and glamour of steam as a British heritage to be proud of, Tourist Board grants are barred. Restoration of exhibits is not regarded as capital outlay by the Tourist Authority.

Readers who have come along with me thus far will be disappointed if I end the Bressingham Steam Story on a complaining, pessimistic note. Earlier on, my more usual optimistic nature should have been detectable, and indeed, I have often taken Mr Micawber's attitude to problems which appeared to be insoluble. Here then is the place to adopt it again, to believe that ways and means will emerge by which steam at Bressingham can be kept alive long after its originator has become but a memory. It is my firm intention never to give in, to try every means possible to ensure its continuity. And to enjoy it, along with others who come to share it, for as much time as there is left to me.

Footnote: After lengthy negotiations with the Rank Organisation which took over Butlins assets, the four locomotives on permanent loan described have been purchased outright.

In addition the Gallopers have been purchased from Flora.

The Museum also includes exhibits from the Norfolk Fire Service, and is open daily from 10.00 a.m. – 5.00 p.m.

Where it all began . . . the stackyard at Bressingham in 1947.

Full steam ahead . . .